SANCTUARY

SANCTUARY

Residences and resorts by de Reus Architects

Mark de Reus

WITH AN INTRODUCTION BY JOSEPH GIOVANNINI
EDITED BY PABLO MANDEL

ORO
Novato, California

Contents

Foreword

MARK DE REUS

The most intimate of human needs is the home: a sanctuary for our physical and psychological well-being. As French philosopher Gaston Bachelard wrote in his seminal 1957 book, *The Poetics of Space*, "Our house is our corner of the world...it is our first universe.... It is an instrument with which to confront the cosmos."

A well-crafted sanctuary offers more than refuge and shelter from the chaos of the world. It is a personal monastery where the mind unwinds and recharges. It is where we tend to be ourselves, and where we unearth creative inspiration. It is, by definition, a sacred place—somewhere life can be supported and nurtured, where the human soul can thrive.

This sacred nature of architecture is a focus of de Reus Architects. It is why, after more than fifteen years as a firm, we still work in the relatively narrow arena of designing homes and resorts, places where people live and play. Recently, we have designed a series of beachfront cottages in Maui, a house high up among the trees in Costa Rica, and a home low in a mountain valley in Idaho, among many other domestic projects.

Wherever it is located, our work is marked by certain qualities. For one, our designs are clear and direct responses to their places and climates. They indicate that what we create belongs to the site and has not been imposed upon it. Stylistically, our work is pluralistic, but minimalism, restraint, and the evocative use of natural materials are prevalent in it. We clearly order and carefully sequence space in all our works. We design a continuity of experiences, rather than a series of episodic events, where the judicious use of transition spaces eases movement from one area to another. The result is a harmonious, layered composition that, above all, is livable. As a prominent interior designer once told me, "The homes you design have souls."

For us, the concept of luxury homes is entirely contextual. We derive our ideas not only from a place's historic forms and environmental considerations, but also from local crafts, methods, and materials. While we often explore how these influences can be used in new ways or adapted to new contexts, we never lose sight of where they come from. We search for a sense of crafted elegance or quiet resolve in this transformation. To us, luxury is not a commodity—not a heroic architectural gesture—but a richness of experience that stems from a design that befits and is tethered to its place.

Our designs are also a product of how we work. Over the years, our practice—which is headquartered in Sun Valley, Idaho and operates two studios in the isles of Hawai'i and Maui—has been developed and refined. Our firm has a collegial atmosphere where critique and new ideas are encouraged. We work methodically but operate informally. Our methods are the antithesis of those of a large corporate architecture firm.

Over time, we have honed our sensibilities and methods, striking a balance between practice and theory. We have developed a craft-based approach to our design process, which, in many ways, has come to feel like a series of rituals. As Finnish architect Juhani Pallasmaa wrote about architecture studios in *The Thinking Hand* (2009), "A unique sense of purpose and order usually resides beneath the seemingly chaotic mess of sketches, working models, materials samples, photographs, notes, memos and books."

With every design initiative, our first order of business—the initial ritual—is to verify the design brief and its requirements. This includes analyzing both small and large patterns of anticipated use. We learn about our clients' routines, and we delve into understanding how they will use the home, both every day and on occasion. We explore how a room's purpose might evolve between day and night. We identify passive and active areas, uncovering where moments of quiet can be found—perhaps inside a room meant for meditation or a study designed for concentration.

Our focus then turns to understanding the specific site: terrain, location, climate, culture, sun and wind, flora and fauna. Here, patterns emerge—like those of weather and drainage, or light and shadow—and anomalies stand out. While our work is often built in varied (and often extreme) climates such as the mountains of the Pacific Northwest and the tropical regions of Hawai'i, Mexico, and the Caribbean, our deep, instinctual respect for the land and its natural systems gives initial shape to our design.

The requirements laid out by the land, context, and client combine to inform site planning and the floor plan. This is usually the juncture where the design concept emerges. The plan, after all, is the most unifying component in any architectural work; it reflects the essence of the main idea of the project and integrates anticipated patterns of living, functional use, and sensory experience into a single design. It is underpinned by a sense of order and structured geometry designed to fit with the natural terrain. Iterative studies and refinements of the plan—both rational and intuitive discoveries—then push it toward its final form.

At this stage of the design process, we pay special consideration to negative or in-between spaces and their impacts on both livability and the occupants' sensory experience. The merging of interior and exterior spaces, in particular, has a direct bearing on one's connection to the site by bringing nature to the user and adding dimensionality to the space. For example, covered terraces offer the comfort of refuge and prospect, the tangible benefit of controlling direct sun, and the occasion of a gracious atmosphere. Much like the long-held Japanese design concept of "borrowed scenery," where far-off landscapes appear seamlessly integrated into an immediate garden, the confluence of layers of nature and living spaces in our projects form a whole greater than the sum of their parts.

Our approach to such layering, of course, hinges on climate. For instance, our Big Wood Residence in Sun Valley, designed in a contemporary ranch vernacular, allows the eye to access as much of the surrounding views as possible, while still prudently using glazed openings to maintain thermal integrity and conserve energy. In the tropics, views play an equally important role in our designs (properties assigned to our trust tend to be blessed with wonderful views), although striking the necessary balance between aesthetics and practicality is made easier here by the simple fact that these environments are often more forgiving. In places like Hawai'i and Mexico, proper shade and plenty of ventilation often make for a pleasant living environment. Not so in Idaho, where the harsher climate makes the handling of sun and shade a more complex question.

In the tropics, the architecture of water is especially meaningful. For architects, water is integral in developing design concepts. It has form and structure; it can be active or passive, static or dynamic. Throughout history, it has understandably played a role in gardens and buildings both for its symbolic potency—as the source of life—and for more tangible reasons. Water's surface, whether still or unsettled, plays with sunlight, adding dimension and atmosphere to a space when reflected against an interior surface. The sound of moving water relieves tension and releases helpful ions. Water's thermal qualities can even cool the air. In our Kauhale Kai Residence, a raised, circular water-filled pool of dark gray basalt sits below an opening in a trellis. It is the axis mundi of the home—a symbolic center connecting heaven and earth.

Details such as this are not conceived at the onset of a project. Invariably, we evolve our designs through layered refinements. For example, we develop a sketch concept on the computer to explore rough building forms or massings. We then translate these ideas into simple physical models that allow for further studies of scale, proportion, the degree to which the interior and exterior can be merged, and other architectural elements. Windows, doors, and other wall openings are studied for how they capture views, day lighting, and ventilation and how their proportions affect the composition of masses and surfaces. Gradually, we layer materiality and textures with modulation onto 3D renderings, which eventually give us a true-to-life sense of the building. All these steps are part of the evolution of an idea becoming a fully resolved design.

Underpinning this entire process is our search for the authenticity of the architectural experience. When a space is encountered and experienced, a dialogue between a user and their environment occurs. It is a multifaceted interaction. Their body feels the space. Their memory is stimulated. Their tactile senses explore the perceived balance and harmony of the composition. This authenticity that we always pursue is existentially meaningful architecture, where the layers of a design are resolved to a singular well-crafted work that rises above function to be nurturing, sustaining, life-enhancing—to be a sanctuary.

After forty years of practicing architecture, the fulfillment I derive from designing and crafting sanctuaries, whether homes or resorts, is as rewarding as ever. Our rituals are still being honed, and our appreciation for architecture's ability to enrich the human experience continues to deepen.

Architecture in Medias Res

JOSEPH GIOVANNINI

The practice of architecture, like politics, may be local, but architect Mark de Reus has always been intellectually itinerant since the beginning. Over the decades, his migratory career has taken de Reus—born and raised in Idaho and trained at the University of Idaho—halfway across the world and back. Friedrich Nietzsche wrote about *Perspektivismus,* about seeing and interpreting reality from many points of view, none yielding a single truth. De Reus has practiced multipersectivalism architecturally. His inquisitive eye has led him beyond the application of a unique design signature across projects to a practice based on versatility, to solutions generated by the basic conditions of a project—what he calls "first principles."

De Reus earned his architecture degree in 1977 at a time when the modernist world of architecture as framed by Le Corbusier, Walter Gropius, and Mies van der Rohe was being challenged, and the canon being expanded. Robert Venturi had published *Complexity and Contradiction in Architecture* in 1966, making way for an architecture that was more pluralistic than the heroic modernism of its legendary founders. In architecture school de Reus encountered Ian McHarg's 1969 book, *Design with Nature,* a book that catalyzed the environmental movement and advocated the integration of the sciences, arts, and planning in a holistic, ecological vision. *Design with Nature* has remained an abiding influence on de Reus throughout his career.

By 1984, when he began what would become a decade of practice in a San Francisco firm, the ecological lessons of Sea Ranch, a seismic architectural event on the West Coast, had fully entered the blood stream of the profession. In 1965, a group of architects—including Charles Moore, William Turnbull, and Donlyn Lyndon—with landscape architect Lawrence Halprin started construction on an ecologically sensitive collection of individual condominiums carefully fitted into the slopes of a windswept plane overlooking the Pacific. Their site planning considered prevailing winds, sun exposure, view corridors, and land conservation. The ethos of the project was humble: shed roofs, wood cladding, and a charming architectural humility borrowed from the vernacular—local barns and outbuildings—that had always respected nature and the environment. For the young architect, Sea Ranch was as influential as Venturi.

San Francisco gave de Reus practical experience across a wide range of projects, from resorts and restaurants to entertainment and residential complexes, but Spanish colonial, the default style favored by developers at the time, bored him into looking for more challenging opportunities. San Francisco pivoted the architect to Asia.

In 1994, de Reus joined an American firm in Jakarta, Indonesia, that worked on resorts. Given his entrance to the architecture profession at a time of increasing pluralism in the United States, de Reus was receptive to alternative architectures. But nothing prepared him for his epiphany at the Amandari Hotel in Bali, where he stayed on a business trip in 1990. "It was transformative," he recalls, "like seeing Ronchamp for the first time." The hotel, designed by Australian architect Peter Muller, was like a village of thatched-roofed cottages. Rather than conceive a hotel as a block of repetitive rooms extruded from a plan, Muller designed a village of pavilions nestled in a hillside of coconut palms. The pavilions stood opposite a village of houses in an intimate valley. "You couldn't tell where the village stopped and the resort started," recalls de Reus. Built with indigenous materials, the post-and-beam architecture with open walls merged with the environment. The design cultivated breezes that aired open spaces under the big, sheltering, hipped roofs that were the buildings' primary features. The pavilions did not exceed the height of palms. The architect had decided to build in a humble rather than controlling or dominating relationship with the landscape. He might have been reading Ian McHarg.

The Amandari Hotel, removed from industrial resorts processing visitors on a conveyor belt of elevators and corridors, eschewed the trope of industrial tourism in

favor of the cultural authenticity of a vernacular architecture crafted with indigenous materials. Its pavilions were basically open room-sized verandas that individuated travelers, setting them in their own gardens. The architecture suspended time and cultivated serenity. Each pavilion was a meditation on nature within the sanctuary of tranquility.

For de Reus, the architecture he encountered in Southeast Asia was not simply exotic. He did not see the buildings as a cultural tourist from the West who would take a snapshot. The buildings weren't objects. The architecture did not speak about itself but looked into nature from nature.

During his five years in Indonesia, he made some twenty trips to Bali. There he found a building and design tradition dating from the refined Majapahit culture (which peaked between 1300 and 1500). Building traditions from that golden age of Indonesia persisted in a regional form specific to Bali for centuries, even into the modern era, removed from the rush of modernization in Jakarta by a jet. De Reus found architecture of gardens and water, crafted from natural local materials, producing an environment of ecological agreement that supported Bali's indigenous fusion of music, the arts, gardens, and painting. "Kids on the street carved sculpture from pieces of wood almost as an act of meditation," he remembers. "They played gamelan, sitting on the floor. Creativity in all the arts was a way of life, integrated, on an everyday basis."

The fundamental unit of Balinese architecture was a single detached structure with a prominent roof, often hipped, that defined its profile and acted as both parasol and umbrella in the tropical weather. Corner posts supporting the roof freed the sides from any structural role while allowing breezes to pass freely through the space sheltered by the roof.

De Reus's epiphany was an open secret shared by other architects, starting with Geoffrey Bawa, a leading modernist who had worked in Sri Lanka and Southeast Asia using local materials and techniques and overhanging pitched roofs. De Reus studied the tradition firsthand, at his own initiative, during both work and private trips around Southeast Asia. In Phuket, Thailand, he encountered the exquisite Amunpuri Resort, its pavilions designed with the cooling effect of adjacent pools and the arching silhouette of Thai temples, which added an element of ineffable grace. The trips amounted to a second architectural education, through an osmosis of place that allowed him to absorb new architectures. In Vietnam, de Reus also encountered charming buildings from the colonial period, but he remained focused on the architecture of indigenous cultures because he found vernacular architecture, rooted in ancient traditions, more inspiring. "The more rudimentary structures bring you closer to the elements," he says.

He also traveled to Japan, which, despite the heavy Chinese influence on its buildings, retained a tradition of tropical architecture since the Japanese archipelago in subtle ways echoed and extended the island and archipelago cultures of Southeast Asia and the Philippine Sea. Independent and culturally inquisitive, he moved between different geographies and climates, absorbing divergent architecture cultures. The larger world was his college, an extension course in continuing education.

The overthrow of President Suharto in 1998 destabilized de Reus's practice in Indonesia. He returned to San Francisco then settled in Hawai'i, where he worked for several years with a firm specializing in resorts and planned communities. In 2005 he set up his own practice in the low-key town of Waimea on the Big Island of Hawai'i.

As it was in the middle of the Pacific Ocean, Hawai'i seemed to put de Reus equidistant from both Western and Eastern influences. But the islands, after being so deeply colonized and Westernized, offered few traces of a native architecture and ancient culture. De Reus's exposure to the indigenous architecture of the tropics in Southeast Asia—including Melanesia, where massive stones were used as foundations—proved a deep well of inspiration from which to draw in a comparable tropical climate. His interest in vernacular architecture has never caused him to abandon

modernism, partially because his conception of modernism was never based in the mechanical—crisp edges, industrial materials, and components serially produced. His is always a softer, warmer modernism that he calls "transitional," which he often builds in wood.

However, even more important than the idea of transportable, adaptable precedent is de Reus's application of what he calls "first principles": design derived directly from the demands and conditions of a project, including its site and culture, rather than adapted from a precedent. The first principles of designing in Hawai'i involve integrating a building with its environment to immerse people into its facts and pleasures. For de Reus, architecture could offer an immediacy of experience. Like a dramatist, he could plunge people in medias res.

De Reus embarked on designing a series of houses and resorts based on a model of pavilions built with natural materials. He set these in gardens spotted with pools and ponds in immediate apposition to porous, open-air spaces that inhaled the out of doors. He eliminated hallways and corridors and placed sliding doors and windows in disappearing walls opposite each other for cross ventilation. Breezes skim the water to air-condition the pavilions. The buildings are subordinate to or coordinate with the gardens, which are designed with the same level of care as interior spaces.

His design technique is deliberate and incremental. After consulting with his clients, registering their needs and wishes, he builds a design up in layers, starting with an assessment of the site—its orientation, views, size, and shape, and, not least, its often-prescriptive building codes. He proceeds to the plan, but not just the plan of the buildings; he plans the whole site so that the outside and inside are integrated into a continuous whole carpeted in grass. In Hawai'i, the roof of his pavilions is the most expressive component of the design, with many variations possible on the basic hipped shape—but all accountable to concerns about shade, rain, and the microclimates they establish.

In his search for an architecture that is an authentic response to a place, he uses natural rather than synthetic materials—stone, wood, and metal—all playing off each other in complementary juxtapositions. He details these with simplicity that emphasizes the essential over the decorative. He then orchestrates all the layers into a symphonic whole, into an agreement from the site to the materials to the detail. His Gesamtkunstwerks never lapse in tone or ring a false note that breaks the environmental spells he creates.

The skill de Reus acquired first as a young journeyman makes this all possible. Before college, he worked in construction across several trades, and as a young architect he designed and managed projects, small to large, for a busy firm. Counterintuitively, what makes his interest in the elements successful is his technological expertise and skill in construction, which anticipate and mediate all the problems of a tropical climate. He designs vacation houses that breathe in the outside when occupied, but that resist humidity for parts of the year when they are vacant and closed. His primary objective is to deliver his clients to the experience of nature. He fuses house and landscape in an environmental equilibrium designed to induce a sensuous response. The houses blend seamlessly with the weather, sky, ocean, and view by opening so completely to the larger environment.

Greene and Greene—early-twentieth-century Arts and Crafts architects whom de Reus admires—worked for years designing cottages in California derived from the bungalows of the foothills of India. They built on their own inventions until they constructed what have been called "ultimate bungalows"—the Gamble House and the Blacker House, for example. In Hawai'i, de Reus evolved and perfected his idea of a village of pavilions in a gardened landscape. His Kauhale Kai, a complex on a double property overlooking Kauna'oa Bay, and the later Ancient Ponds Residence on the south Kohala coast, qualify as "ultimate hales." Here he invented, developed, and perfected a type that displaced clichés of Hawaiiana

that had been built for decades with a grace and authenticity of its own. Built on the Big Island in planned developments with design guidelines, each is a consummate summary of tropical island traditions cast in the form of a family village. The commissions had the land, views, budget, and client confidence requisite for realizing a complete synthesis of de Reus's interpretation of tropical Southeast Asian architecture.

Both villas are collections of freestanding rooms, with independent guest and bedroom clusters surrounding the main gathering space, itself an ensemble of pavilions. The organization offers privacy in the separate buildings but community in the open public rooms and the lawns, which are themselves a commons for the village. Predicated on cultivating Hawaiian paradisiacal pleasures through design, the houses are resorts that integrate open-air leisure with an indoor-outdoor complex. Their design responds to the environmental gentleness of the islands with its own architectural gentleness. Breathing space, light, and air, the pavilions are, in a way, transparent to the garden, seats within the wide panorama of Hawaiian nature.

In music, the silences between notes reveal the sounds around them, and in these two projects, open courtyards are spatial silences binding the many pavilions into a house conceived as a community of individual buildings. Each of the buildings is treated as a freestanding hale, or a small cluster of hales, fitted with separate or joined hipped roofs. The relationship between the outside and inside spaces is reciprocal, each complementing and defining the other. Some of the courtyards are pools or reflecting ponds, while others are landscaped gardens. Some pavilions, bordered by water, appear to float like boats. Hawai'i-based landscape architect David Tamura designed the landscapes as outdoor living spaces: emerald lawns reveal the undulating contours of sites spotted with foxtail palms, which add the grace of their curving trunks and feathery fronds to the environment.

De Reus centers the living and dining areas on the property, putting the separate guest cottages at the site's edges and cultivating gardens and paths in the space in between. Most of the pavilions have glass walls that slide back to open the interiors directly to the out of doors and to the pleasures of the Hawaiian day and night—breezes, sunlight, shadow, fragrances. With sliding glass walls, the interiors become facades displaced to the inside, a visual condition de Reus backstops with solid and elemental materials: travertine, coral, cedar, teak, and ohia.

The defining form of each pavilion is its roof, which acts both as parasol and umbrella. Roof shapes are for de Reus a territory of invention. At Kauhale Kai the roofs are pyramidal, while in the Tropical Residence they relax at the edges. In both project, roofs rest on solid, coral-stone clad columns for support. For Western eyes attuned to the regularities of modernism, the structural clarity is familiar, comfortable, and literate. The clean detailing owes a debt to the disappearing details characteristic of the modernism of his formation. The honey-colored cedar undersides of the hipped roofs step down with the slopes. Light bouncing up off the warm marble floors causes the stepped wood ceilings to glow.

In these elegant pavilions, de Reus has hybridized his own background, conflating his early interest in transitional modernism with his informal education in Southeast Asia. The crisp lines of the coral-stone clad columns and details reveal that he never abandoned the modernism in which all architects of his generation trained, before integrating other influences. Throughout these homes—because of materials, detailing, craft—there is a sense of luxury without any display of luxury. The villas become part of the nature that their design cultivates and reveals; the two merge into a tapestry of pavilions and gardens viewed through pavilions and gardens. De Reus has built a sense of aloha that once typified the Big Island's tradition of ease and welcome—that you can relax into a benign environment that somehow takes care of things. The luxury is the sense of sanctuary.

De Reus individuates each house in plan, detail, and materials. In the Tropical Residence he roots the house in

the landscape by tightly fitting irregularly shaped blocks of lava into piers that ring one of the terraces into a Hawaiian Stonehenge. The wall of stone creates a protected outdoor space for an entry garden, allowing glimpses through spaces between the piers from an exterior court. Terraced pools at the ocean side of the property step down to the lava beds, recalling the terraced landscapes in Asia. One pool offers an opportunity to swim at a transition point between the grass and the lava field, between cultivated and found nature.

In the Bias Residence, de Reus adds another layer of culture to his modernist hales: Japan. There are many versions of tropical architecture, and arguably they include buildings in the Japanese archipelago. Deeply associated with China culturally, Japan nevertheless reflects Oceanian traditions. When de Reus visited Japan, spending a week in Kyoto, he recognized architectural affinities to Southeast Asia in post-and-beam structures open to the out of doors under substantial roofs operating as parasols or umbrellas. The temples handle tropical humidity by inducing breezes.

What fascinated de Reus, however, was the Japanese use of sliding or perforated screens that gave spaces the possibility of closure, privacy, or semiprivacy, not to mention the functional flexibility of easy room reconfiguration. The clients of the Bias Residence had visited Japan as well as Bali. When de Reus designed their house on the Kohala Coast, he integrated elements of Japanese architecture—porous wooden screens, some sliding—that defined smaller spaces within larger areas while letting space and breezes flow. He basically grafted Japanese screens onto the vernacular architecture of post-and-beam construction common throughout the tropics. "They act as sunscreens to the outside, but inside as transitional devices between spaces that can create privacy," he says.

At the entry gate, de Reus introduced one of the multiple voices of his integrated architectural conversation with the point, line, and plane of an early modernist De Stijl composition. It acts like a torii entrance gate but takes on an abstract modern form: a white stone column supports a black roof plane and a pivoting black metal door, next to a thin line of steel. From here a long stone walk of basalt pavers ambles along a stepped diagonal down the middle of the long property, its jagged stepped edge bordering a shallow pool on one side and a garden on the other. The path leads to an entry to a house without an apparent front door: the outside flows to the inside with a barely visible barrier. A pool of water next to the stone entry path slides below the flat overhanging roof, flowing water into the house, as though the house were simply a transitional zone between the nature on one side and the sea of lava and ocean on the other. Overhead, to accommodate solar panels, de Reus flattened the hipped roofs.

De Reus's modernism and his tropical vernacular have simplicity and functionalism in common, and the styles meet and complement without conflict in a house where, beyond the entry, Japanese screens veil spaces. He, however, didn't start designing the Bias Residence with a style in mind. As with all his projects, he started with the land—here a long, wide parcel. Set like a green island of lush lawn in a black sea of surrounding lava, compound gravitates to the property's edges, as though to the hull of a boat. The whole site is like a field of dynamic architectural play and interchange rather than a lawn centered on a house. Instead of pointing views straight out across the surrounding field of lava to the ocean and the horizon, de Reus oriented the pavilions on a bias to the property line for a view that strafes the coastline.

Despite the impression that the flat roof gives at the entrance, the spaces inside the Bias Residence open to the shallow underside of a long, hipped roof surfaced in clear teak, calling to mind Frank Lloyd Wright's interiors. But if Wright grounded his houses around the fireplace, the hearth here is an expansive pool that helps structure the plan, giving the house orientation. At the side of the open dining and living area leading to the pool, steps lead into an inlet of the pond (where depth varies from four to nine

feet). On the other side of the inlet, the stone floor leads to a seating area fitted into the pond. "My client asked for a dining pavilion floating in a reflecting pool," de Reus says. The square of space, under a hipped roof, is an island.

The house lives in the landscape. The floor plan slides its occupants into nature. An allée of six palm trees gives a geometric order to the yard; the trees lead from the beach side of the house to the living area, where two other pairs of palms cross the allée. Next to that crossing is the spatial pivot of the house—a raised fountain under an oculus cut into a wood trellis above. In a house that ambles episodically across its site, a circle in a trellis open to the sky atop a circle of water establishes a vertical axis. It connects sky and water in an axis mundi found in some Asian architecture, including China's temples.

De Reus's architecture literacy crosses cultures, and the Bias Residence is perhaps the most Eurasian of his houses. Here he has crossed an ocean and continents through centuries of architectural history to distill a design that, with great ease and no architectural pretention, draws on tropical architecture, Japanese interiors, Frank Lloyd Wright, and traditions of modernism, all while ultimately surrendering to the Hawaiian landscape with timeless grace. Pool, house, and lawn lock into an experiential continuum that fuses outside and inside. A masterpiece of formal composition, material harmony, and cultural synthesis, it delivers the reason for being in Hawai'i: nature.

For de Reus, one lesson of his peripatetic career has been openness to the many ways to look at shelter. His formations on both coasts of the Pacific have elasticized his range of architectural responses. He is not an ideologue on a mission professing a single approach. His expansive view of architectural styles, which embraced the tropics of Southeast Asia and Japan, started much earlier in his career. As a student he was interested in the transitional styles of the early twentieth century in the San Francisco Bay Area and Southern California—the work of Bernard Maybeck, William Wurster, and Greene and Greene—as well as the shingle style from the East Coast, reintroduced and reinterpreted by Robert A. M. Stern.

De Reus began his career with an expansive curiosity and interest, so when a couple came to his Hawaiian office requesting a vacation home designed in an Arts and Crafts style, he honored the request. The style envisioned by his clients, an architecture of enclosing walls, was counterintuitive to his practice—pavilion architecture with the exfoliating perimeter of post-and-beam structures. For de Reus, the Ancient Ponds Residence "could have been a home built in Hawai'i a hundred years ago": its style of walled solidity already "belonged" to the island historically.

As usual with de Reus's work, the design started with the site, which here featured anchialine ponds, ancient pools of shallow water where Hawaiians once raised fish. The ponds, in all their wild irregularity, are beautiful, haunting, and protected by statute. "The edges of the ponds and their required setbacks left room for a tortured building envelope," says de Reus. "Luckily an Arts and Crafts house can be flexible, because it's not rigid in its formal massing and roof design."

De Reus not only had to fit the footprint of the house within the organic contours of a site edged by the ponds, he also had to comply with roof height restrictions. The site and height restrictions resisted geometric regularity, but brought out the informal possibilities of an Arts and Crafts building to amble episodically around and through the site, like a village of attached buildings. De Reus segmented the hipped roof to change direction with the plan. He absorbed the idea of anchialine ponds into his site by designing a swimming pool that is virtually indistinguishable from the ponds themselves.

The architect opened the house to the exterior, making a transition between outside and inside, with generously sized, roofed lanais. Its perimeter beams are supported on wooden wishbone arches—knee braces—springing from stone piers. De Reus continues the knee-brace detail inside along the two-story entrance corridor, where

arches spring from squinches to support a wooden truss that in turn supports a pine ceiling under the ridge of the hipped roof. The coral stone walls, travertine floor, and wood arches, beams, and trusses structure the house in a visible display of craftsmanship. De Reus leaves the wood natural; the interior has the rich, warm feeling of a cottage. Louvered door panels covering sliding glass doors deliver breezes. A collection of antique ship mastheads brings Hawaiian maritime history into the house.

Many of de Reus's commissions involve generous properties that encourage designs that sprawl across a landscape that folds back in indoor-outdoor floor plans. The villas become equal parts land, water, and house. However, the site for the Ancient Ponds Residence did not allow sprawl but forced the five-bedroom house into a second story. Using the Arts and Crafts language, designing a house of stone walls under a gabled roof, de Reus created a house in a transitional style that recalls a period of innocence, circa 1910. In most of his hale villas, he treats sites like a checkerboard of yard and structure, while here, he breaks open the two-story volume of the house by lapping the swimming pool up to the lanais that edge the house's ocean-side perimeter. Upstairs, balconies hooded under roofs edge the perimeter, creating more transitional space between outside and inside. De Reus sustains the Arts and Crafts ideal inside with ceilings crafted in woods or detailed with wood trim.

In 2015, de Reus began revisiting and refreshing the Four Seasons Hotel on O'ahu's rugged west coast. The modern, high-rise structure was the kind of building he had worked on early in his career, before his epiphany in Bali and before he set up his own practice. It was designed in 1989 by Edward Killingsworth, a Los Angeles architect who had participated in the famous Case Study House program of the 1950s and '60s. A master of small- and medium-scale work in Southern California, Killingsworth practiced architecture at a bigger scale in the Pacific basin. There he built many large resort hotels, including the seventeen-story O'ahu project, which was a model of clarity, structural expression, and formal abstraction. The hotel exemplified the kind of building that was Manhattanizing the island.

The new owners wanted to refresh and even rephrase the property. In its time and for its size, the hotel represented enlightened commercial work, and de Reus accepted its architectural clarity and respected its integrity. In his design he aimed to mitigate its impact on the landscape and to humanize its interiors, from the lobby to the guest rooms. He took a soft approach to a hard building.

The Four Seasons overlooked a man-made cove and beach that made ocean water accessible on an otherwise rocky coastline. It was sited next to one of three artificial lagoons built along the coast, and de Reus ingratiated the hotel into the landscape by stepping terraces and swimming pools down to the lagoons, hyphenating the hotel to its site's key feature. He basically performed a heart implant on the outdoor space, giving the complex a lively piazza where a choice of pools invited kids. Adjacent to these terraces, a new outdoor deck extends an existing restaurant, populating an underdeveloped part of the site that profited from the view. De Reus refreshed the old and tired travertine hardscape with basalt paving. Set in a herringbone pattern, it gives the decks rhythm and a quiet energy. On the side of the hotel facing the ocean, he developed a quieter outdoor precinct featuring a long, wide pool set next to a lounging deck intended for adults.

At the perimeter of the building, de Reus introduced a more human scale to the modern original. He skirted the base of the tower with low pavilions and outbuildings whose hipped roofs and woodsy casualness connect the tower to the landscape and reference an informal Hawaiian culture. New details also bring the human scale to the building. Carved figures inspired by Pacific Island sculpture and made by a local artist populate the grounds in and around the porte cochere. Wall-to-wall carpets woven in the patterns of indigenous baskets are placed in guest rooms. Wooden ceiling fans laze overhead. De Reus broke the chill in the marble lobby by adding wood

frames to openings and by paneling the reception area in teak decorated with an art piece derived from fishing nets. He replaced the long reception desk set at the bottom of a vertiginously tall seventeen-story atrium with pods to encourage a more intimate welcome. Though it was impossible to change the massive building in its architectural fundamentals, it was possible to change the culture of the hotel, to bring Hawai'i in. De Reus's strategy was not decoration per se but affirming the experience of nature and O'ahu's welcoming culture, which brought travelers to the hotel in the first place. Bringing out the ecology of the site was part of the design strategy.

De Reus designed a chapel at Four Seasons. With a simple gabled roof and a wooden belfry, it recalls the nineteenth-century churches established on the island by missionaries. He kept the exterior simple and rudimentary but opened the interiors with wide expanses of glass in divided window frames. The front wall's large arched window delivers congregants to a long view of the ocean. Often used for weddings, the chapel brings views of nature to services of all types. "I wanted the inside of chapel to be humble and straightforward," says de Reus. "I used painted wood, reverse board-and-batten wood walls, a rustic oak floor, and Shaker-style wood benches." A master of tone even when the architectural assignment is modest, he knew which materials and furniture to call on to create a mood.

Many of de Reus's villa complexes are located in controlled developments with design covenants. But in 2016, he was given a comprehensive commission to design all the buildings in a twenty-four-acre coastal property, the Mākena Golf and Beach Club. Although the club, featuring two eighteen-hole golf courses, didn't aspire to achieve the density of a hotel, its ambitious mix of apartments and villas challenged the integrity of the Hawaiian landscape.

De Reus's did not choose to design all the building types within the project in a single style. Rather, he used a range of architectural approaches, some leaning toward the tropical, others toward modernism. All emphasize an architecture that keep the homes open to views and receptive to Hawai'i weather, while sustaining the environment with careful building placement.

The first architectural installment on the site is the Mākena Beach Cottages, a compound of nine two-story, four-bedroom houses. Clustered in a double row, they face a common green and a beach, with a view to islands across the water. The 3,800-square-foot houses—each on a long, relatively narrow parcel—are more compressed than de Reus's typical villas that incorporate outdoor spaces between pavilions. These houses are clustered with an intimacy that fosters a sense of community within the enclave. The occupants of the houses are neighbors who share a common lawn, pool, and the beach beyond.

In designing these cottages, de Reus started with a characteristically Hawaiian hipped roof. In the early 1900s, the Dickie roof—a shallow hipped roof flattened at the edges to increase shade—took hold in cottages built across the islands, and de Reus recalls that tradition. The luminous green-turquoise color of the first-story walls evokes the sandy, white-bottomed shallows of Hawaiian lagoons and coastal pools. Visitors are unmistakably on the islands, not in a Los Angeles suburb.

On the ground floor, de Reus merges dining and living spaces in an open plan. He organizes the upper floors around a central corridor. A pair of hipped roofs covers four second-story bedrooms, two on either side of the corridor, all gaining height from ceilings open to the roofline. Sliding glass walls open major rooms, including the upstairs bedrooms facing the ocean, to covered patios or terraces overlooking a private yard with a pool and small lawn.

The design combines the spatial intimacy of a town house with the indoor-outdoor porosity of de Reus's Hawaiian villas. The Dickie roofs signal the Hawaiian inspiration of the houses, but the language otherwise is one of modernist simplicity designed to amplify the environmental pleasures of a tropical house. Like the early modernist

styles he admired, styles between styles, the design of the Mākena Beach Cottages is transitional.

De Reus's task in designing the master plan of the Mākena Golf and Beach Club was to keep the landscape open—without challenging the environment with overwhelming building footprints—and to encourage a casual island ethos. He clusters freestanding houses in relatively compact areas and designs apartments in two-story buildings sited in other areas. At the center of the project lies a clubhouse, with apartments on a second floor. He sites each component on landscaped terraces that follow the natural slope of the hillside toward the water. To diversify the architecture and avoid monotony, de Reus designs each part of the resort in a style best suited to its task and location. The diversity reflects the diversity of buildings on other parts of the island, so that the club does not look like a gated community set apart with an elitist style.

The club itself (about to start construction at the time of this writing) is a two-story courtyard structure stretching across the site parallel to the beach. Its flat, modernist roof accommodates solar panels that help power the building and permits views to the water for other structures built up the slope behind it. Guests enter the club at the upper level of a structure that steps down with the site twice, leading to a terrace with swimming and wading pools that act as the social center of the clubhouse.

Beyond the clubhouse, on the upper terraces of the site, de Reus locates a two-story apartment complex. Spacious open-plan interiors and double-height entries greet residents with the generous spatiality of lofts. Here de Reus explores height and the Z dimension in ways that his single-story villas do not permit. Again, de Reus stresses the primacy of experience, designing walls with huge sliding glass doors. He cultivates the sensuous character of the apartments through a heightened tactility, choosing open-grain oak for the floors, stairway, doors, and surrounds. He uses sustainable wood on the second-floor facade and board-formed concrete on the garden fences.

The versatile de Reus commands a fluency across styles, whether he designs Arts and Crafts houses, Southeast Asian–inspired villages, modernist hotels, or vernacular buildings. Within the context of his culturally and environmentally tactful designs, one surprise does stand out in his portfolio. In 2017, he designed the seven-bedroom Coral House, in construction at the time of this writing, well beyond the transitional modernism to which he has gravitated since his student days. Here he ventures into heroic modernism, producing a strong piece of architecture that would be at home in a mainstream history of modernism (though it would not be permitted in most planned developments in Hawai'i).

On a windy site on Maui, he translated his post-and-beam wood-frame architecture into a steel-and-glass structure. The house fronts the entry with a remarkable transparency that sends the eye straight through it into the far landscape. Inside, an open plan turns the interior into a minimalist landscape that flows through plate-glass walls to the outside. A flat roof with dramatic cantilevers rises toward the view, throwing the eye into the distance while protecting the glass walls and the interior from the tropical sun and rain. The rising roof creates the impression of an exaggerated forced perspective.

The back of the house advances and recedes, wrapping around a courtyard with a pool to incorporate the out of doors into its volume. All rooms are double sided for double exposures. The virtuoso design reveals that a modernist substratum to de Reus's sensibility informed even the most vernacular of his buildings, giving them a clarity that enhances the traditional idiom.

On Hawai'i, de Reus's designs bring out the paradisiacal potential of vacation sites, but in Mexico's Los Cabos corridor on the Pacific Coast, he cultivates an ecological utopia. He nests the Chileno Hillside Villas within a lush jungle of palm trees on slopes surrounding a small bay. His models were villages and towns like Positano on the Amalfi Coast, whose houses and footpaths spill down hillsides toward the water.

De Reus terraces the houses into the hillside, connecting them with stone footpaths to create a pedestrian village. A lower and upper street crosses the hillside. Each unique house is surrounded by a natural garden, offering a view of the bay and proximity to the native vegetation of its Edenic location.

As the famous German naturalist Alexander von Humboldt, the "inventor of nature," discovered in the early nineteenth century, ecosystems at the same altitudes in the same latitudes are similar. Though his discoveries in botanical geography were largely made in mountains on different continents, he might have made the same observation about architecture in the tropics. Conditions in Southeast Asia can be found on the other side of the Pacific in another hemisphere, with similar architectural consequences. For example, the pavilions of Southeast Asia have equivalents in Hawai'i (hale) and in Mexico (palapas).

Palapas, simple post-and-beam structures with sheltering roofs made of thatch, are adapted for the Chileno Hillside Villas not just because they are culturally evocative. Their form helps houses in the resort to minimally disturb the hillside, sustaining the existing landscape. The development focuses on a center of palapas that house a reception area, dining commons, spa, library, bar, and pool.

The project takes place within a social and cultural ecosystem that includes local craftspeople working with local materials. The resort confirms and helps sustain an existing social fabric. Unlike many Hawaiian building materials, necessarily imported because of shortages on the island, all of the Chileno Hillside Villas materials—stones, thatch, even the plaster on concrete walls—are common, if not indigenous. They are crafted by local workers who have for generations built structures in the tradition that de Reus's design affirmed. The stone used in the footpaths and floors came from Mexican quarries. Spectacular stone walls with complex patterns are fitted and laid by local masons. A public patio boasts retaining walls fitted with irregular stones in a textured pattern, and big, water-worn boulders found on site are integrated as features of the landscape. Woods are largely local and curated for dimensional stability over time.

A bar set among curved pools is an exceptional piece of design. Like that of other palapas, its structure is a four-poster supporting a hipped roof. Here de Reus chose swaybacked mahogany trunks, each wrapped in strangling vines, and dowelled them at a listing angle into large, round boulders serving as a foundation. The bar is a tour de force exhibiting a trunk's desire to lean, as though seeking sunlight. The unequal lengths of the trunks tip the roof, lifting it at one corner, creating a disobedient angle that confirms the palapa's organic quality that ignores Euclid. The expressive, sculptural form tells a story about nature, growth, life, and competition for the sun in the jungle.

Chileno Hillside Villas' communal dining room and lounge, with roofs taken to a monumental scale, are also supported with tree trunks wrapped in strangling vines. They harmonize with the environment they support and give the sense that they grew out of the landscape that they occupy.

After nineteen years of practice on the Big Island, de Reus opened a second office in Ketchum, a mile from Sun Valley, where he and his wife could live in a place that offered the skiing and fishing he grew up with. It was a different kind of paradise from Hawai'i, one with seasons, and it is a destination of choice for many people. Those who build homes in this location are looking for sanctuaries—here, in the bracing cold. Hawai'i was not in itself an ideology for de Reus, but a place where he had been able to cultivate an expertise he had acquired over decades, applying Ian McHarg's lessons about building with nature. The same lessons could be applied in the mountainous West.

From its beginnings in San Francisco, de Reus's practice had always been inquisitive rather than doctrinaire, and as he circled the Pacific Rim he had put his ear to the ground and listened. Instead of importing the architecture and

attitude of a different or alien culture, he respected the traditions and spirit of a place, and embedded his designs in its character and circumstances. Each place had its own culture, which had grown from the nature in which it was embedded. What was unusual about his international practice was that he knew how to respond and ground a design in what was local while cultivating what was elemental and therefore universal.

In Idaho, his first project was his own house, the River House. De Reus found a seven-acre property in Blaine County at the foot of Carbonate Mountain. As usual, he grew his design out of the site and local culture. Despite its large size, the plot's buildable area was only one-and-a-half acres—and irregular at that, after avalanche and riparian setbacks, floodplains, and shepherd's easements were subtracted from the total. De Reus's design needed only 3,600 square feet. It also needed the consent of his primary client, his wife, who liked pared-down simplicity but not modernism per se.

The permitted area paralleled the river and faced a grove of aspen trees within a larger riparian forest at the foot of the mountain. The property had a front, the point of arrival off the road, and a back, with the Big Wood River running through it. The site favored a long and narrow bar-like structure that, in its pared-down simplicity, took on the visual character and profile of a barn under a gable roof. De Reus wasn't drawing on historical precedent for the sake of tradition but recreating a typology that happened to grow out of the site conditions.

"Out of deference to nature, I wanted to find the right scale, something that was modest and appropriate for a riparian forest," he said. "I like agrarian typologies, and a simple rectangle reflected the form of a barn." He had found the shape by induction, the same way he discovered the hale as an appropriate form in the tropics. The logic that had led de Reus to an architectural simplicity in pursuit of environmental fundamentals also led him to spare, clean, undecorated shapes and surfaces of a vernacular building type that had an affinity to the spare, clean, undecorated shapes and surfaces of modernism. The vernacular and modernism shared a relationship with simplicity.

The succinct scale of the two-story barn-like shape, however, couldn't contain the whole program of a 3,600-square-foot house, so he simply stapled a single-story, flat-roofed structure to the main form to accommodate cars, storage, and an entry vestibule. He placed the kitchen in the virtual overlap between the two structures, which allows it to be entered from two directions.

Louis I. Kahn, who defined buildings as either "served" and "servant" spaces, would have identified the low structure as the servant space to the barn. A covered outdoor terrace, situated at the rear of the house in the geometric overlap of the one- and two-story structures, acts like theatrical seating for the spectacle of the aspen grove and the mountainside rising beyond it. Stained dark gray, River House's wood siding complements the vivid colors of the aspen trees as they shift through the seasons.

Clean and crisp, the barn is modest geometrically and clean-cut volumetrically. The interior is effectively a modern cabin with a rusticated oak floor. White pine walls and ceilings clearly define the geometric volumes. Detailed with the minimalism of an art gallery, the interior nonetheless has a rustic warmth because of the wall-to-wall, floor-to-ceiling pine. De Reus combines the kitchen, dining, and living areas into a single space focused on a blackened steel fireplace with a granite hearth, which takes up the whole wall opposite the kitchen. At night the house glows with the warmth of a cabin in the woods.

Nature was the real client of a house in the Lakeside region of Tahoe, which de Reus designed from his recently established office in Ketchum. The site has a hillside view on the east shore of Lake Tahoe. De Reus's design grew from a cabin that once stood on a natural bench in a sloping landscape of ponderosa pines and cedars, some 150 feet tall. The footprint of the old cabin gave the new structure its scale. To keep the house from sprawling into the landscape and occupying more land on this sensitive hillside, the house acquired a second story. In the tropics, de Reus's houses sprawled into the landscape, maximizing the ratio of surface to volume; Yellow Jacket did the opposite, gathering itself into an efficient and succinct two-story volume that could maintain rather than lose its heat in the Alpine climate. The architect was not applying a style developed in one climate to another. He derived the form suggested and required by the climate.

De Reus connected the roadside garage and auto court to the living areas on the second floor via an elevated footbridge that finds its way to the front door without displacing any pines or disturbing the ground plane. Using stone in the lower level of the facade, redwood siding, and two-story tree trunks as columns, de Reus integrated the house materially into the forest as part of the environment, "so as not to overwhelm things, to stay architecturally quiet," he says.

The perimeter is an active edge that meanders in and out of Yellow Jacket's volume: outdoor spaces carve into the volume, and terraces project into the canopy of surrounding trees. The simple ribbed gable roof floats serenely over an intricate facade, taming the complexity in deference to the simple, rustic houses nearby. The gable roof suits Tahoe's heavy snow loads. Natural materials—patinated natural zinc, black-stained wood siding, clefted limestone, exposed steel, and tree trunks used as columns—ground the design in a material authenticity. As in de Reus's villas and resorts in Hawai'i and Latin America, this house displays perfect pitch for the snow country of the West. De Reus bases his response in nature, the climate, local traditions, and, of course, client expectations. The house belongs to its undisturbed landscape.

What appears to be luxurious is simply nature at its most natural. Here in Yellow Jacket, as in his island homes, de Reus never interposes self-conscious design between the building and nature. He cultivates understatement to drive complexity into simplicity, and to deliver his clients into environmental sanctuaries, in medias res. Translating nature into a building demands discipline and craft at the service of a vision.

In disciplined acts of architectural modesty, with the lightest of touches, de Reus holds back from spectacle and from signature. Nature itself seems to be the architect who designs in an Edenic equilibrium between man and nature. Deftly, discreetly, sensitively, de Reus seems to have simply provided a roof.

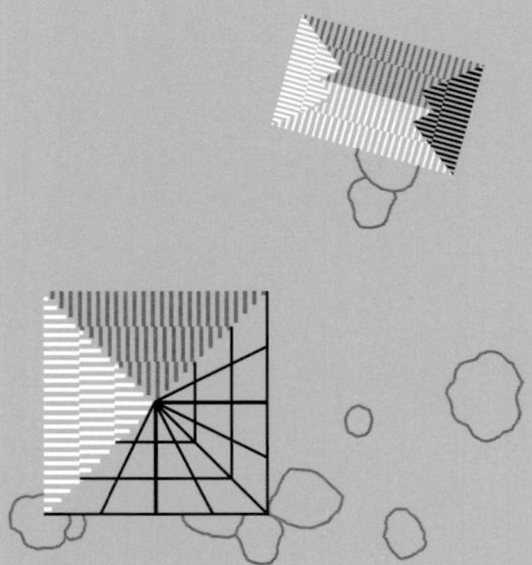
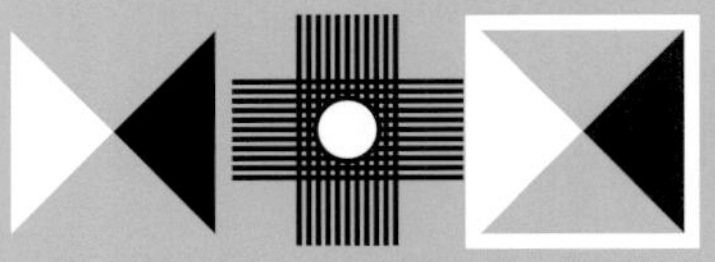
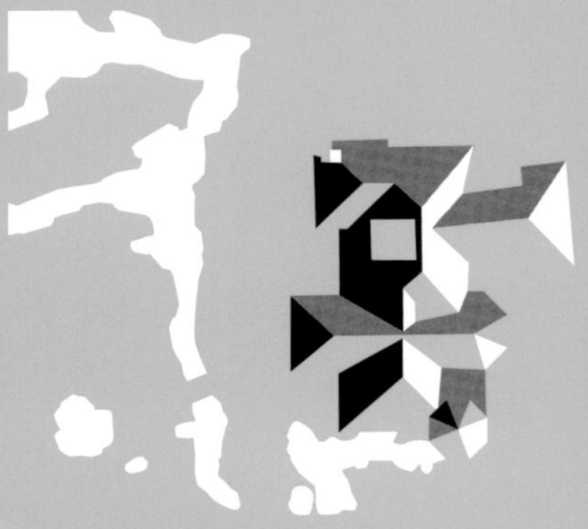
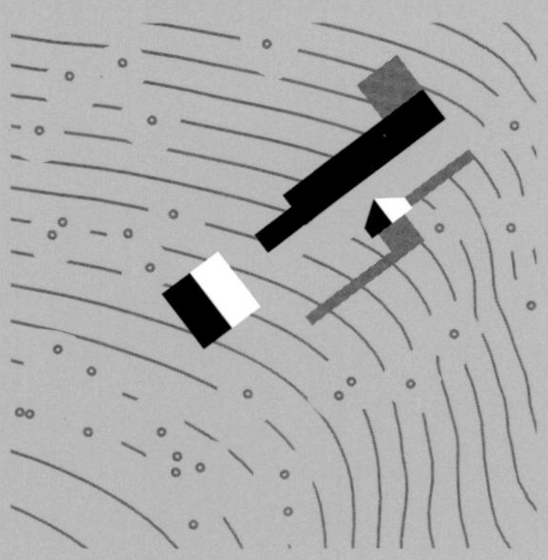

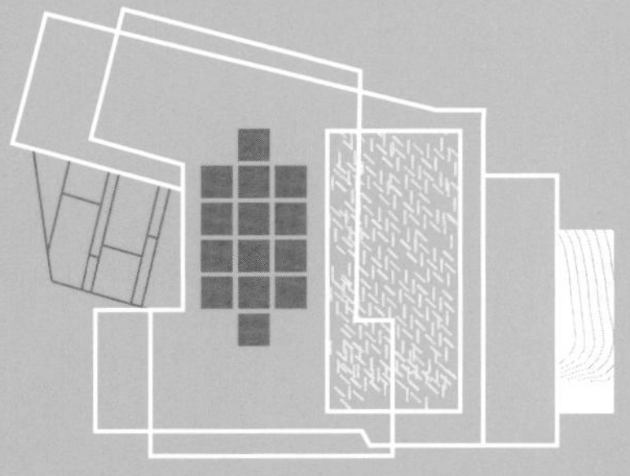
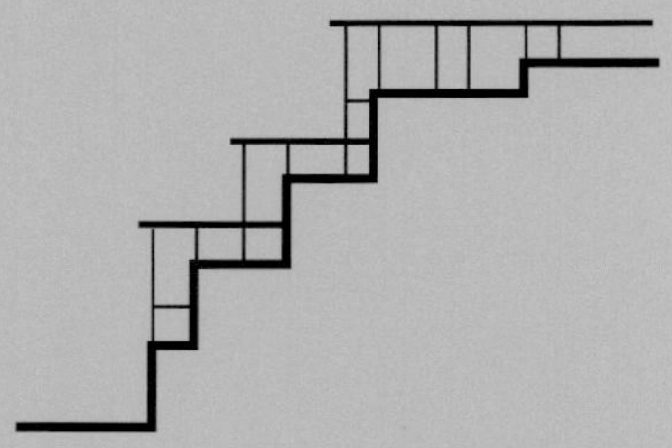

Works

Kauhale Kai Residence

SOUTH KOHALA, HAWAI'I

This private residence within the Mauna Kea Resort property on the island of Hawai'i was a longtime dream of its client, who fondly recalls family vacations to the famous hotel nearby. The husband and wife shared an affinity for Hawai'i and Polynesia, for modern art and design, and for the beauty of natural materials and craftsmanship.

On a site overlooking the Pacific Ocean above Kauna'oa Bay, this home aspires to connect to the spirit of Polynesian cultures. A series of modern tropical pavilions positioned on the property proffer the sensibility of home as a village. The residence's hipped roofs are the most visible expression of its organization. They are used because they are a strong tropical archetype that fits this coastal community's design guidelines requiring traditional building forms.

The site plan expresses an idealized diagram of spatial order. It allows the best tropical livability from the property, as it merges outdoor and indoor living. The experience of living amid the pavilions and gardens is shaped and influenced by water. One enters the property through a secluded gate and is greeted with a water feature of large, stacked stones in a circular pool. This stone wall functions according to feng shui principles and allows the view of the ocean to unfold gradually. The sound of running water adds a cooling affect. The stacked stone wall was inspired by the megalith stone ruins in the Micronesian island of Nan Madol, Pohnpei.

Alongside the entry, a dining pavilion floats in a reflecting pool that flows into a lower swimming pool, designed for its architectural presence and lap swimming. The lower pool is the armature or organizing element for the arrangement of pavilions, terraces, and lanais. At the center of this arrangement is a raised circular water feature on axis with the lower pool, with an overhead trellis connecting the dining and outdoor pavilions. This is the axis mundi of the home: the symbolic connection between heaven and earth. A circular hole in the trellis directly over the raised pool of water is an aperture to view the night sky.

A play of contrasts creates artistic tension throughout the design of the home: asymmetry against symmetry, the rustic alongside the refined, and the casual with the formal. Just behind the axis mundi, the main gathering pavilion is a single space with living area, kitchen, and open pantry. This pavilion is connected by a breezeway to the garage and laundry. The outdoor living pavilion echoes the stepped-ceiling forms and columns of the dining pavilion. These are reminiscent of the Majapahit culture of Bali. The primary pavilion houses study, bedroom, sitting room, dressing areas, indoor bath, bath garden, and view lanai. Outside this pavilion, on axis with the pool, an antique Balinese door is framed by Hawaiian basalt stone. Two guest pavilions, each with two-bedroom suites and a living area, reside on the east side of the property.

Exterior materials include copper shingles, steel doors and windows, integral-color cement plaster, cedar wood eaves, coral-clad columns, and travertine pavers. Durable low-maintenance materials were selected for this tropical coastal marine environment. Solar panels are located out of sight atop the garage pavilion. Interior finish materials include cedar ceilings, local ohia hardwood cabinetry and floors, sand-grain veneer plaster, travertine stone, and teak hardwood doors.

Site concept sketch

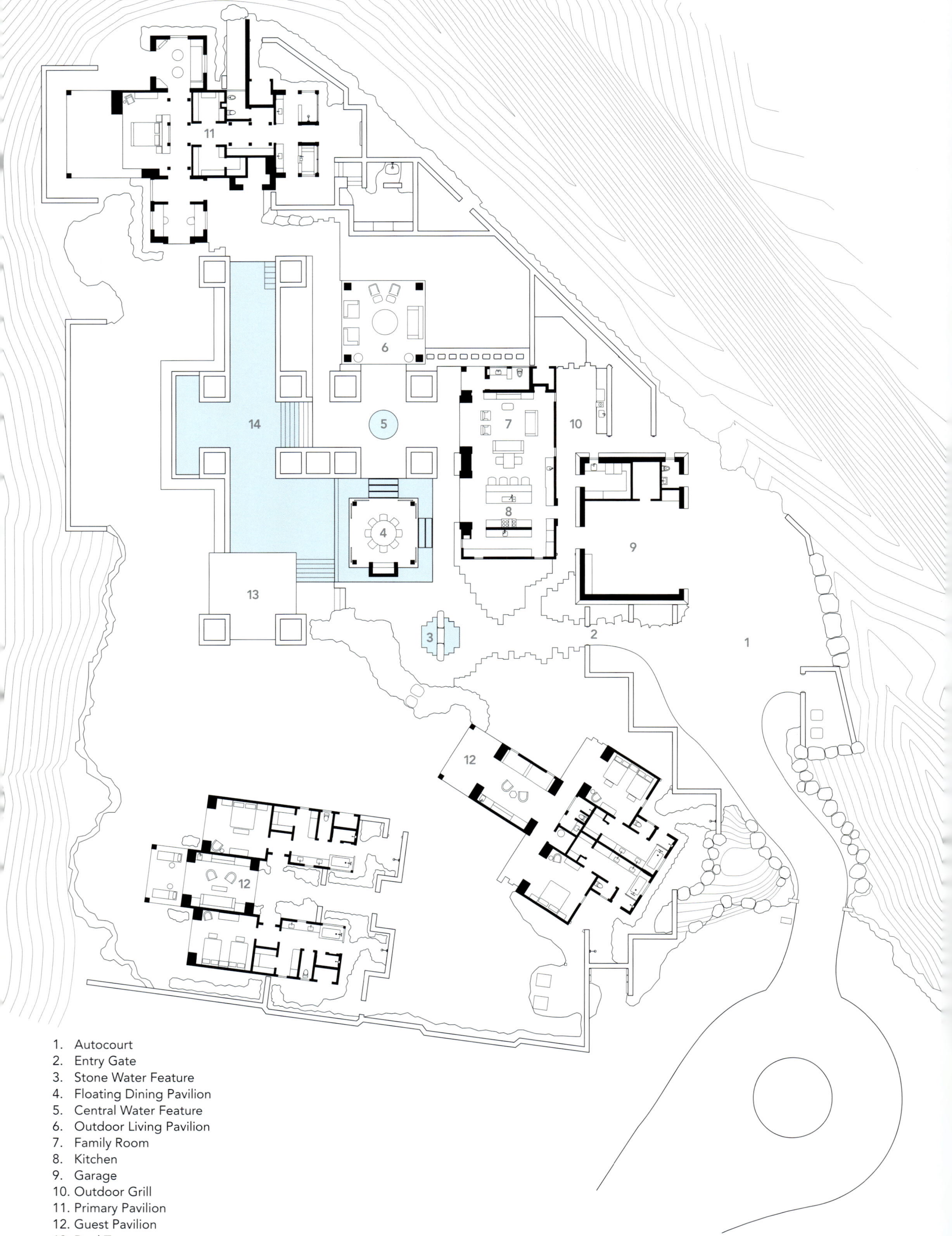

1. Autocourt
2. Entry Gate
3. Stone Water Feature
4. Floating Dining Pavilion
5. Central Water Feature
6. Outdoor Living Pavilion
7. Family Room
8. Kitchen
9. Garage
10. Outdoor Grill
11. Primary Pavilion
12. Guest Pavilion
13. Pool Terrace
14. Pool

The home orients to views of Pacific Ocean with Kauna'oa Bay in foreground and Haleakala on Maui beyond.

A stacked stone water feature along the entry path to the home was inspired by the ancient megalithic stone structures from the Micronesian island of Kosrae.

A shade trellis connects the outdoors with the dining pavilion.

A circular trellis opening rests above a raised stone reflecting pool that serves as the axis mundi—the symbolic connection between heaven and earth—of the home.

A reflecting pool surrounds the dining pavilion.

A linear lap pool sets up a geometric axis along which the pavilions of the home are organized.

The pool's basalt stone side walls have a small recess to receive the water surface.

The gray plaster pool bottom reflects a deep lagoon-like blue of the sky.

The reflecting pool surrounding the dining pavilion spills into the swimming pool.

Stone steps connect the dining pavilion.

Stacked-stone water feature at the entry.

An elegant tautness is achieved with the copper metal roof shingles on the hipped roof.

Stone bases are detailed to receive the steel trellis posts.

Cedar wood is used on ceilings and roof eaves.

Stepped cedar wood ceilings of the outdoor living and dining pavilions are inspired by the Majapahit culture of Bali.

Local Hawaiian Ohia Lehua hardwood is used for all architectural cabinetry. Kitchen and bar counters are of black granite.

Interior wall finishes include coral stone and integral-color cement plaster.

Teak hardwood posts form a strong axial relationship in this hall within the prime bedroom.

The headboard is white bronze detailed with a Polynesian motif.

The interior designer displayed the owners' collection of Tahitian seashell necklaces.

The Art of the Pacific Islands

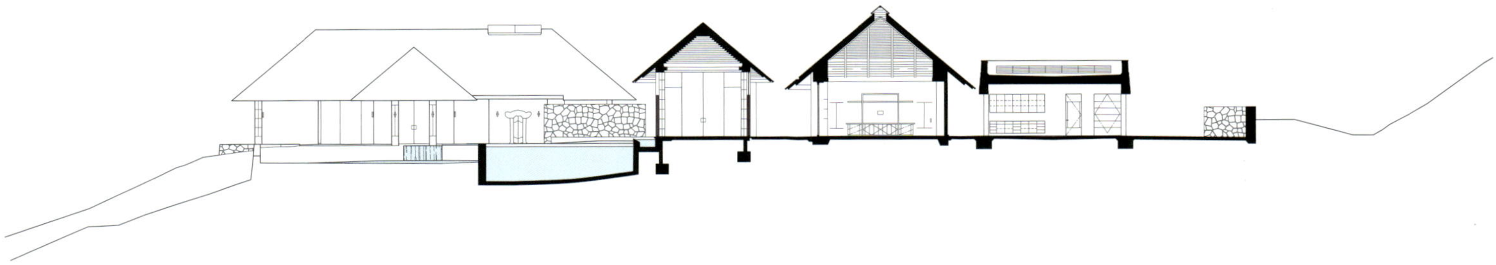

Site section

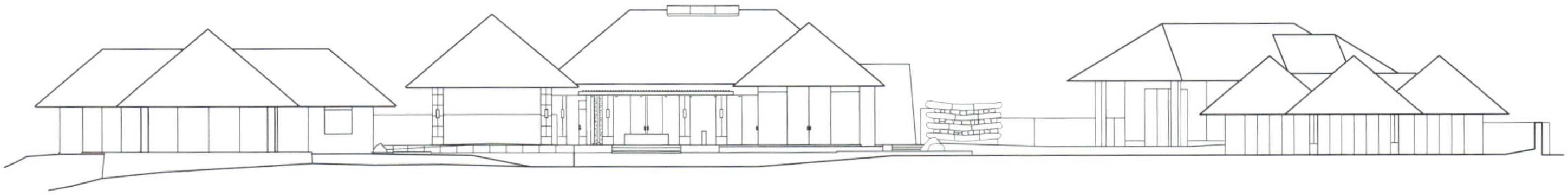

Elevation

The dining pavilion appears to float in the surrounding reflecting pool.

The dining pavilion with kitchen behind.

A collection of antique ceremonial Balinese Kris daggers and handles are displayed on a coral stone wall in the dining pavilion.

Big Wood Residence

SUN VALLEY, IDAHO

Local vernacular and a minimalist concept drove the design of this home, situated just south of Sun Valley, Idaho. This residence for Mark de Reus and his family sits in an aspen forest alongside the Big Wood River below Carbonate Mountain on a seven-acre property.

The vision for the home was one of a simple barn with the feel of a modern cabin on the inside. The living areas are within a two-story gable form, and an engaged flat-roofed structure contains the garage, storage, and terrace. Within the 3,760 square feet of living space, the living room, kitchen, pantry, and primary suite are on the ground floor, and recreation room and two bedrooms on the second. A glass-enclosed vestibule forms the eastern entrance; it is designed to appear like a warm welcoming lantern on a dark night. A tall window alongside the vestibule lets morning light into the main living space. Large windows on the west side of the home provide views of the mountain and forest toward the river.

The design has a simplicity that belies its complexity and effects a modern barn and cabin atmosphere. The project's black stained wood exterior and dark gray metal roof harmonizes with the color of the aspen forest. Rusted steel fascia are at the flat roofs and steel columns at the terrace. An interior palette of finish materials was selected for the modern cabin aesthetic: rustic European oak flooring, grayish pebbled granite stone floors and counters, and walls, ceilings, and cabinetry of eastern white pine with a light finish that shows the grain but protects the wood from ultraviolet light. A blackened steel fireplace wall anchors one end of the main gathering space, the open kitchen the other end.

Detail appointments include a glass and steel handrail at the stair, flush reveals around interior doors, flush pine cabinetry designed for a minimal modern appearance and function, illuminated glass cabinets and open shelves for display, a cantilevered steel shelf for a Balinese Singa sculpture at the steel fireplace wall, and a window seat in the daughter's bedroom.

Lighting includes a cast-glass dining light pendant by Alison Berger that reflects the site's history as a place where block ice was cut from the river. Kitchen-island light pendants designed by Swiss architect Peter Zumthor are minimalist appointments. Tech Element recessed lights are the predominant ceiling light fixtures, and integrated lighted mirrors are used in bathrooms.

Site plan sketch

1. Main Gathering Area
2. Dining Area
3. Kitchen
4. Primary Bedroom
5. Primary Bathroom
6. Powder Room
7. Laundry Room
8. Patio
9. Guest Bedroom
10. Guest Bathroom
11. Rec Room
12. Garage
13. Spa

Second level floor plan

First level floor plan

The home sits within an aspen forest alongside the Big Wood River below Carbonate Mountain.

Steel posts support the roof over this outdoor terrace. A fire element is surrounded by a steel plate capping a concrete pedestal.

A simple palette of white pine for ceilings, walls, and cabinetry is used with granite and rustic oak floors throughout the home.

Light pendants designed by Peter Zumthor reinforce the minimalist aesthetic of the home.

VENETIAN
PALACES

A blackened steel fireplace wall anchors an end of the main gathering space.

An antique Balinese singa statue rests on a cantilevered steel ledge at the fireplace wall.

A study and recreation room is between two bedrooms upstairs.

The stair is detailed with a glass-and-steel rail.

The prime bath with granite floors, shower walls, and counters.

The dining pendant is designed by Alison Berger with Holly Hunt. The fixture's design concept of quarried ice tied in well with the past use of the nearby natural springs that supplied ice to the Sun Valley Lodge.

Bias Residence

SOUTH KOHALA, HAWAI'I

Alongside an 1801 lava flow on the leeward coast of Hawai'i, this residence was designed as modern island architecture that connects the owners to nature and Polynesian culture. The home's living spaces orient toward glancing coastal views, which is counterintuitive to the development's master plan that is directed straight out to the ocean. Aligning the living spaces on the bias to the property lines resulted in a collection of intriguing spaces between the separate pavilions. The spaces of the home are organized as a series of interlocking pavilions and produce negative space—the Japanese concept of *ma*. Low-slope hipped roofs are designed in a contemporary aesthetic and meet the spirit of the community design guidelines calling for traditional roof forms. Flat roofs over in-between spaces allow solar panels to be hidden from sight.

Bias Residence has an undercurrent of a Japanese sense of restraint, and the concept of tropical minimalism is used throughout the home. An antique Taisho era (1912–26) kimono displayed at the entry foyer sets a vibrant tone for Japanese modernism. The driftwood-stained white oak ceiling of the main gathering area was designed as a minimal shelter with long wide planks laid up. Architectural hardwood sliding screens were used as room dividers and for privacy and sun control. An abstracted Japanese geometric pattern was used for the stone backsplash at the kitchen and the stone headboard of the main bedroom. Contemporary pendant lights reference traditional Japanese lanterns.

Finish materials were selected for their natural beauty and durability, as well as for their contribution to the residence's minimalist aesthetic and quiet sense of restraint. Exterior finishes include zinc metal roof shingles, black anodized aluminum doors and window frames, painted steel fascia and columns, integral-color cement plaster, and stone terraces, walls, and columns. Interior finishes comprise stone and teak floors, granite counters, veneer plaster walls, and stained white oak ceilings, cabinetry, and millwork.

Concept sketch

1. Main Gathering
2. Dining
3. Kitchen
4. Entry
5. Primary Bedroom
6. Primary Bathroom
7. Garage
8. Powder Room
9. Guest Suite
10. Guest Bathroom
11. Pool Terrace
12. Pool

Basalt stone pavers patterned to reinforce the bias orientation of the home on the property.

Water gently spills into a reflecting pool alongside the entry door. The stone pathway leads to the motor court.

A restrained palette of design elements: hipped roofs on stone and metal columns, stone walkways, an architectural pool engaged with the floor plan, coconut palms, and lawn, alongside a natural lava field.

Whitish granite counters with a detailed white stone kitchen wall provide a subtle balance with the stained oak cabinetry and ceiling planks.

Convenient pool access is just off the main gathering area of the home.

Teak wood architectural screens provide a quiet veil between entry and the main gathering space.

A curved stone wall, carved from one block of Calacatta marble, forms a shower enclosure in the center of the primary bath.

The primary bath opens to a garden with an outdoor shower under a trellis of native ohia wood.

Teak architectural screens provide privacy and sun control in the primary bedroom.

Yellow Jacket

LAKE TAHOE, NEVADA

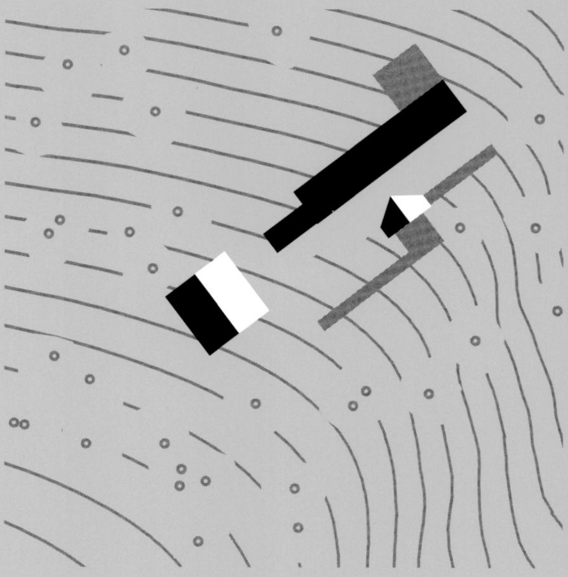

The clients for this family mountain retreat desired a contemporary design that would be in harmony with the predominantly traditional styles in the neighboring resort community on Lake Tahoe's east shoreline. Our intent for the design of the home was to defer to nature and recede into the hillside among the ponderosa pines and cedar trees.

The home is two stories to minimize its footprint and site disturbance. The residence's main gathering areas are placed on its upper level so as to capture filtered views of the lake. Two large split-granite boulders define the entry from the auto court. They lead to an elevated walkway that enables easy arrival from the garage to the front door and the upper living areas. The charcoal gray and black hues of the exterior allow the home to recede within the natural setting of the hillside and forest.

A gable roof supported by paired wood rafters on steel trusses with large overhangs protects living spaces from sun and snow. Selected for their contribution to the architectural concept, durable exterior finish materials include natural patina zinc standing-seam metal roof, cedar wood siding stained black, clefted limestone-faced retaining walls, natural tree trunk columns, and ironwood decks with black steel railings.

The interior finishes and atmosphere complement the exterior palette of finishes with stained white oak wide plank floors, cabinetry, and wood trim. Blackened steel is used in conjunction with clefted gray limestone for feature walls. Interior lighting grazes these walls and illuminates the artwork. Alison Berger glass dining pendants add artistic elegance and softly illuminate the circular Eucalyptus wood table. Cast bronze hardware designed by Mark de Reus and produced by Sun Valley Bronze is used throughout the home.

St. Dizier Design created an interior atmosphere of elegant craftsmanship and restraint in collaboration with the architecture. This was done with the use of select rustic wood walls, artisan furnishings and appointments, a combination of coloration and textures with fabrics and detailing, and incorporation of the client's artwork.

Concept sketches

Ponderosa pine trunks are used as two-story posts to support roof and deck.

A cut limestone wall encloses the fireplace and anchors one side of the main gathering room.

Blackened steel surrounds the openings through the stone wall.

Painted steel railings with an Ipe hardwood rail along the entry bridge and deck.

Fit within existing Ponderosa pines and cedars, the home's footprint is minimized to rest on a small hillside bench where an old cabin was located.

1. Main Gathering
2. Dining
3. Kitchen
4. Powder Room
5. Primary Bedroom
6. Primary Bathroom
7. Garage
8. Outdoor Deck
9. Junior Bedroom
10. Junior Bathroom
11. Laundry
12. Rec Room
13. Guest Bedroom
14. Storage

Lower level floor plan

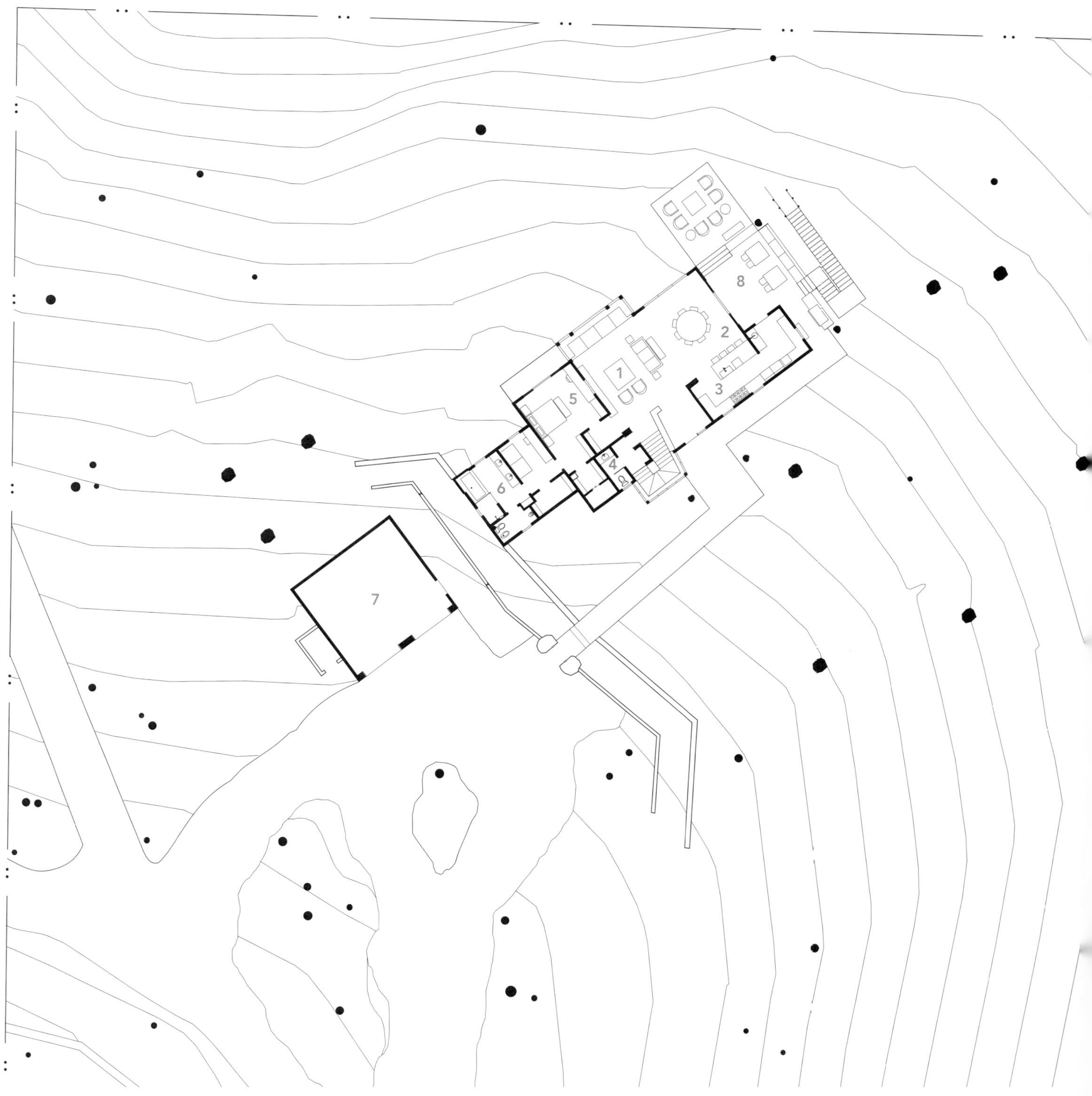

Upper level floor plan

Exterior materials were selected to harmonize with the hillside forest.

Ancient Ponds Residence

SOUTH KOHALA, HAWAI'I

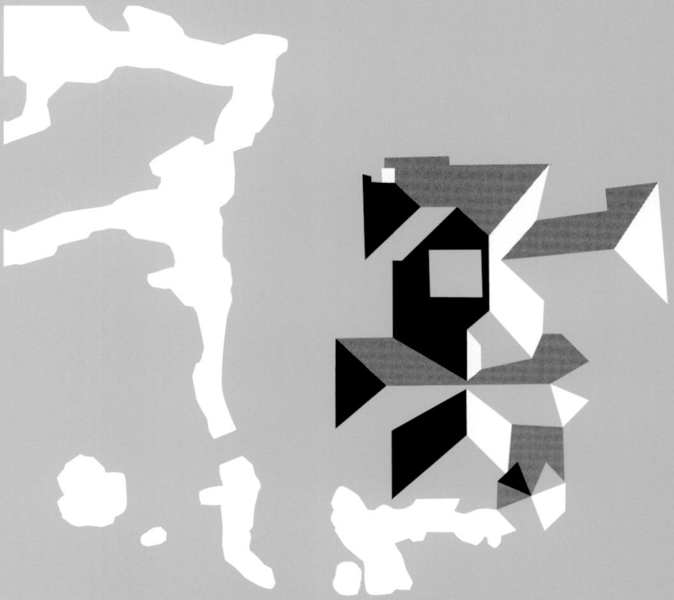

Overlooking coastal anchialine ponds where ancient Hawaiians raised fish, this home for an extended family was designed so that all its major living spaces capture views of Uluweuweu Bay. The design of this home was inspired by the writings of John Ruskin and the Arts and Crafts movement. At its philosophical root, the movement was invested in the essence of the human spirit, utilitarian values, rustic simplicity, and the use of handcraft, natural materials, and allied arts. The owners of Ancient Ponds Residence desired their home to be designed in this same early-twentieth-century spirit to accommodate their contemporary lifestyle.

The dogleg shape of the building envelope reflected setbacks from the anchialine ponds and many building restrictions. But the irregular shape allowed the layout of the home to meander with the ponds. The benefit to this is all rooms have a view of the ocean, and the house feels like an organic part of the land. Much like at traditional Hawaiian homes, here the makai (seaward) side of the home opens as much as possible to the views. The mauka (inland) side has enough windows for ventilation and private gardens.

The main gathering spaces along with the primary bedroom are in the main hale. Guest rooms are in a separate hale across the pool and garden. One arrives at the home at the end of the road by winding through large hala trees and entering a casual auto court. The exterior white coral stone arrival vestibule is compressed to a low scale with a cedar beam ceiling. The entry then expands into a high-ceilinged foyer with timber-frame trusses, leaded glass, and white coral stone walls. The focal point of the foyer is a covered lanai and the ocean beyond. The main gathering areas of dining, living, kitchen, and primary bedroom are reached from this foyer. Transition spaces are a prime architectural element throughout the home. Vestibules, foyers, and lanais add luxurious graciousness to the livability and functionally and provide shade and outdoor living areas.

Natural materials for the home were selected for their contribution toward a spirit of Arts and Crafts ideals, island life, and durability. The soft natural patina of zinc metal used for the roof complements coral stone exterior walls with flush grouting—a masonry approach typical of the early twentieth century in Hawai'i. Teak hardwood doors and windows add richness and warmth to both exterior and interior. Interior finishes consist of local ohia hardwood and travertine stone floors; cedar wood trusses, rafters, and ceiling boards; plaster walls; and teak hardwood doors. The clients' collection of late-nineteenth-century ship figureheads are featured throughout the house.

Arts and Crafts details course through the home: curved timber wood trusses at the foyer, curved wood knee braces in the lanai. Combed cedar wood wallboards, cast bronze hardware, an etched metal range hood, and cast bronze beam fastenings were all designed and selected to evoke the spirit of the Arts and Crafts era.

The landscape design by David Tamura is evocative of old Hawai'i. It includes large endemic hala trees, which are often found around older homes on the coast. Coconut palms were placed as if they grew naturally on the site, and edible plants are near the kitchen. The pool design references the anchialine ponds and is toddler friendly.

Concept sketch

1. Main Gathering
2. Dining
3. Laundry Room
4. Entry
5. Primary Bedroom
6. Meditation
7. Garage
8. Guest Hale
9. Guest Suite
10. Living Room
11. Common Room
12. Pool

Ancient Hawaiian ponds sit between the home and the beach.

A swimming pool is designed in the spirit of the natural anchialine ponds on the property.

Wood timbers, stone walls and floors, and leaded glass are detailed to evoke the home's Arts and Crafts spirit.

The owners' collection of antique masthead figures are integrated into the home.

A painting by Arman Manookian is seen on a stone wall in the entry vestibule.

A curved cedar wood knee brace sits on a haunch of a coral stone pier.

Cedar wood trusses, timber, and planks support the roof of the main gathering rooms.

A view from a small study looking through the stone arch of the lanai out to the beach and ocean.

Cedar wood timbers support a cupola above the meditation room.

Combed cedar wood walls line the casual entry to the kitchen.

Cedar wood ceilings, coral stone walls, hardwood floors, and teak louvered doors comprise the architectural finishes of the primary bedroom.

Punta Sayulita Club and Treehouse

RIVIERA NAYARIT, MEXICO

Located on a peninsula overlooking the Pacific Ocean, the bay, Sierra Madre Mountains, and the seaside village of Sayulita, this thirty-three-acre resort community was created by Contact Development with a vision of sustainability and recognition that success is measured by economic, ecological, and community factors. Creating an appropriately handcrafted and sustainable development within the local and regional community was an integral part of the development vision and guided all aspects of the planning and architectural design.

Planned and designed as an authentically crafted seaside village, Punta Sayulita Club and Treehouse is inspired by traditional vernacular buildings found along the Nayarit coastline. Planning studies determined that sixty-two private residences and a 11,000-square-foot clubhouse would be the optimum carrying capacity of the site. From there, attention was given to integrate the buildings with the hillsides with the least environmental and visual impact. Homes are positioned on the hillsides to preserve drainage and blend into the environment, roadways are sized for carts, and low, stone-masonry retaining walls terrace the hillsides for minimal disturbance. Local woods are used for construction, and dried palm leaves for roofs. Large granite boulders eroded by shoreline waves provide iconic natural character along the water's edge. The project employs xeriscaping to promote water conservation. Residents experience the club as a hillside village offering sun-dappled shade during the day; at night, the stars, lights, and sounds from nearby Sayulita village offer another distinct experience. Buildings are sited to blend with the natural terrain, extant boulders, and protected oil palms. The three hilltops on the property are preserved as parks for the Sayulita community.

Just above the bay's boulder-strewn coastline, the club's amenity spaces are organized in individual palapas (thatched-roof pavilions) and nestled under canopies of oil palms and gumbo-limbo trees, with views of the bay. Four residential prototypes were designed—the Casita at 2,928 square feet, the Casa at 3,467 square feet, and the Casona at 6,148 square feet—to embrace the region's ancient vernacular. Each incorporates local materials and craftsmanship, including thatched roofs, tropical hardwood columns and beams, and wood railings. The two-level, four-bedroom designs nestle into the hillside, with a floating lower deck featuring openings for the trees to grow through.

Site plan sketch

Matapalo tree trunks support the palapa roof of the bar and rest on large granite boulders. The design of the thatched pavilion is purposely imperfect to lean the structure over the pool.

The swimming pool and bar palapa are designed organically into the hillside. The dining palapa is seen beyond.

1
2
3
4
5

1. Club Arrival
2. Club Restaurant
3. Pool Bar
4. Club Fitness
5. Men's Lockers
6. Women's Lockers
7. Massage Pavilion
8. Boat Dock
9. Casita
10. Casa

An intimate stone and grass terrace cut into hillside.

An outdoor shower against a stone wall.

Hillside terraces and pools are formed with local granite boulders.

A well-shaded lawn terrace takes advantage of a hillside ledge.

The arrival palapa has a large stone wall designed with ancient Mayan detailing as a reminder of the site's history.

The bar palapa has low stone walls and local hardwood counters.

The open-air dining terrace has views across the bay to Sayulita.

This Treehouse Villa is one of the residential designs for the club.

The Treehouse Villa has structured interior volumes that merge with the jungled hillside. Materials are local woods and stone.

Tropical Residence

SOUTH KOHALA, HAWAI'I

Natural site features and the unique spirit of the land were incorporated into the design for this private residence along the South Kohala coast of the Big Island of Hawai'i. The architectural design of this home is contemporary vernacular. Blended pitch and hipped roofs are the predominant element giving the home its exterior architectural character. Situated along a rugged stretch of coastline, this five-bedroom residence was designed as a series of separate hales and sited as an oasis within its volcanic landscape. Each building is carefully positioned on the property to capture the drama of ocean waves rolling across the horizon to crash into the lava formations of the coastline. The architectural massing and composition of the main hale arrange the main gathering area—large outdoor lanai pavilion, office, and primary bedroom—under a large roof form. All other spaces—including a guest hale, family hale, and fitness area—are connected via a meandering garden walk. The arrangement of the hales creates a sense of the home as a village and merges organically with the unique high-relief landscape gardens designed by David Tamura.

Ocean and island feature prominently in the experience of living in this home. The ocean is deep along this site, and whales linger quite close to the edge of the island. Within the zone between ocean and home, at the edge of an 1850s lava flow, an organically designed swimming pool creates a destination in the garden and a focal point from the home. The tiered and sinuous forms of the pool design by Tamura effortlessly merge with the lava flow. The idea of water continues in his design with a small natural stream, seemingly coming out from under the home and spilling into a shallow part of the pool. This stream picks up on the uphill side of the home coursing through a lava garden. The main gathering space is designed with large openings on the mountain and ocean side of the space. It is here that the continuity of the garden and the resting between mountain and sea (mauka-makai) presence is experienced. Symbolizing a natural stream, the water connects the house to traditional Pacific island sources of sustainability—the mountains and the sea.

There is a minimalist contemporary aesthetic to the architecture throughout the home. Exposed wood beams at the roof eaves support the taunt skin of the metal roof. The proportions and detailing of the home grew out of the need to harmonize with the surroundings, to eliminate the distinction between interior and exterior, to frame views, and to utilize natural elements. Natural light filters into the interior through large glass pocket doors to create a luxurious atmosphere.

Concept sketch

1. Main Gathering
2. Dining
3. Kitchen
4. Laundry Room
5. Primary Bedroom
6. Primary Bathroom
7. Meditation
8. Garage
9. Guest Living
10. Guest Suite
11. Guest Bathroom
12. Patio
13. Pool

Resting within a reflecting pool, a sea grape tree shades the entry court.

Slits in the surrounding stone walls offer views to the gardens beyond.

The powder room is detailed with a sink carved out of a block of marble. It rests under an architectural screen that gives privacy to the toilet.

Next page: the main gathering room with a teak wood ceiling.

The primary bedroom and its lanai in foreground.

Ohia and teak hardwoods warmly contrast with travertine floors and stone consoles that flank a breezeway between dining and kitchen areas.

A tiered swimming pool rests alongside a coastline of lava from an 1850s lava flow.

The floor of the outdoor living pavilion drops down from main gathering space to maintain views of the ocean.

The landscape architect, David Tamura, designed this lava garden on the mauka side of the home.

The roof of the primary bedroom extends to cover the lanai and provide shade. The interior finishes consist of cedar wood for the ceiling, teak hardwood for the doors and transom, integral-color cement plaster for the walls, and travertine for the floors.

Coral House

MAUI, HAWAII

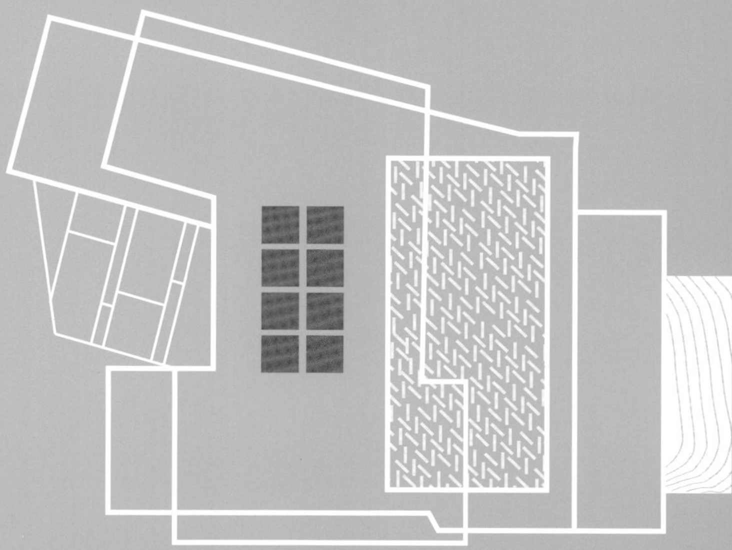

At its heart, this vacation house is about creating a sanctuary where a multigenerational family can share experiences and create memories. Overlooking Maui's southern shore with views to the ocean, mountain landscapes, and other nearby islands, this home was designed to experience nature and support active lifestyles.

The home's architecture is both contemporary and casual, befitting its coastal neighborhood, its intended family use, and a less-is-better approach that results in a minimalist aesthetic and restraint. A strong connection with nature and livability drives the arrangement of Coral House's main gathering spaces. A covered lanai sits between the pool and interior living, dining, and kitchen spaces. Large pocket doors open to merge the exterior and interior spaces. They allow for an open plan with kitchen, dining, and living areas integrated into a single casual space that uses a unified language of material finishes and detailing.

The home's flat roofs are tiered for scale and designed with large eave overhangs protecting the lanai spaces and interiors from sun and rain. Second-story living spaces are set back from the ocean side of the home, due to development requirements, and a green roof provides these spaces with an upper garden and ocean views. Photovoltaic solar panels on the upper roof are hidden from view below. Exterior walls are designed with durable materials such as coral stone walls and aluminum brise-soleil screens providing shade and privacy from the street and neighbors.

Sustainable strategies—including large roof overhangs for shading, green roofs, natural ventilation, metal-clad doors and windows for durability, photovoltaic solar panels and battery storage, a well-insulated building envelope, high-performance glazing, brise-soleil sun screens, ceiling fans to augment natural ventilation, stormwater management, daylighting, use of local ohia hardwood, and energy efficient appliances—resulted in LEED Silver certification.

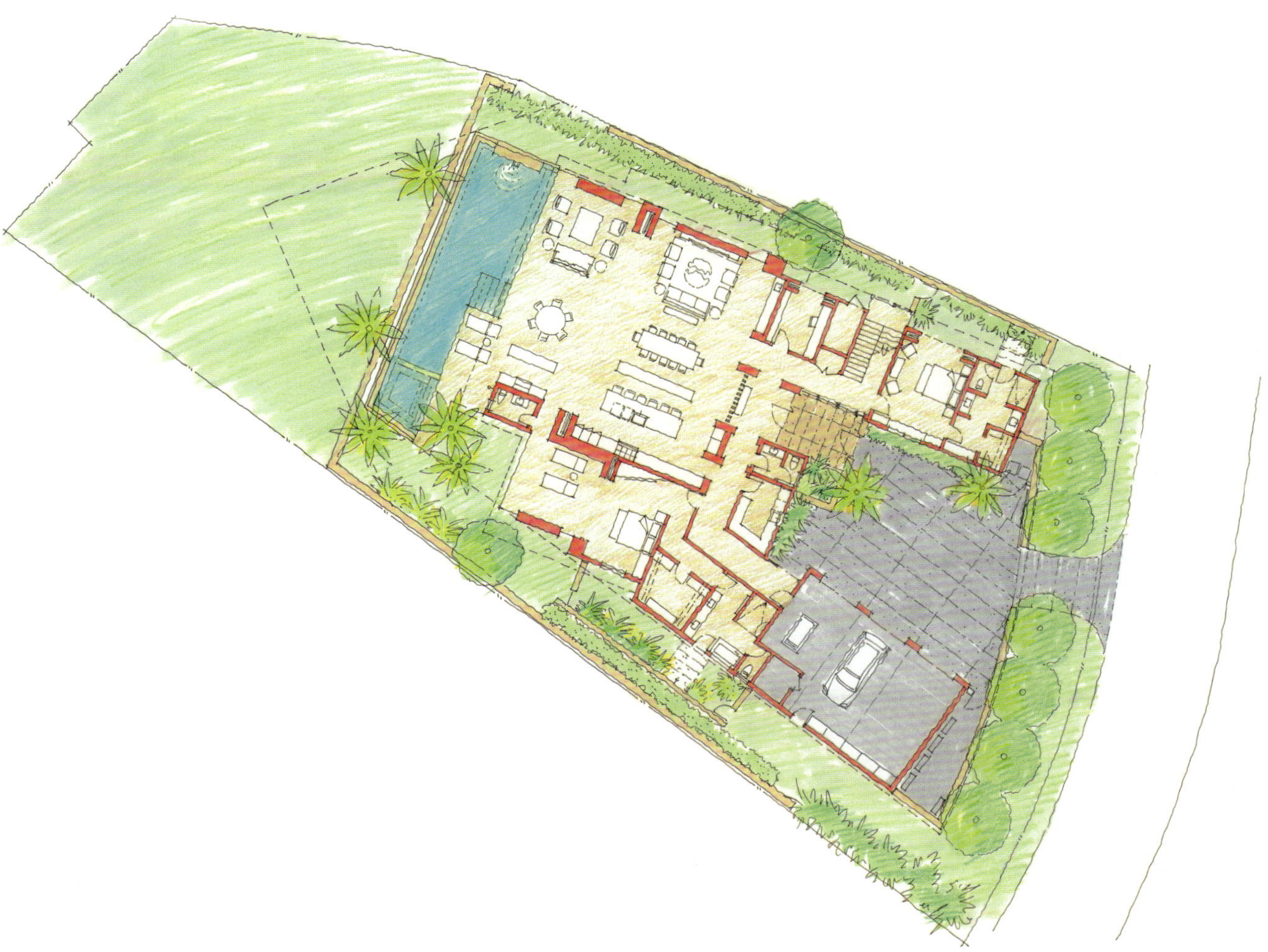

Concept sketch

1. Dining
2. Great Room
3. Kitchen
4. Laundry Room
5. Entry
6. Primary Bedroom
7. Office
8. Garage
9. Guest Bedroom
10. Guest Lanai
11. Pool
12. Lanai
13. Spa
14. Rec Room
15. Green Roof

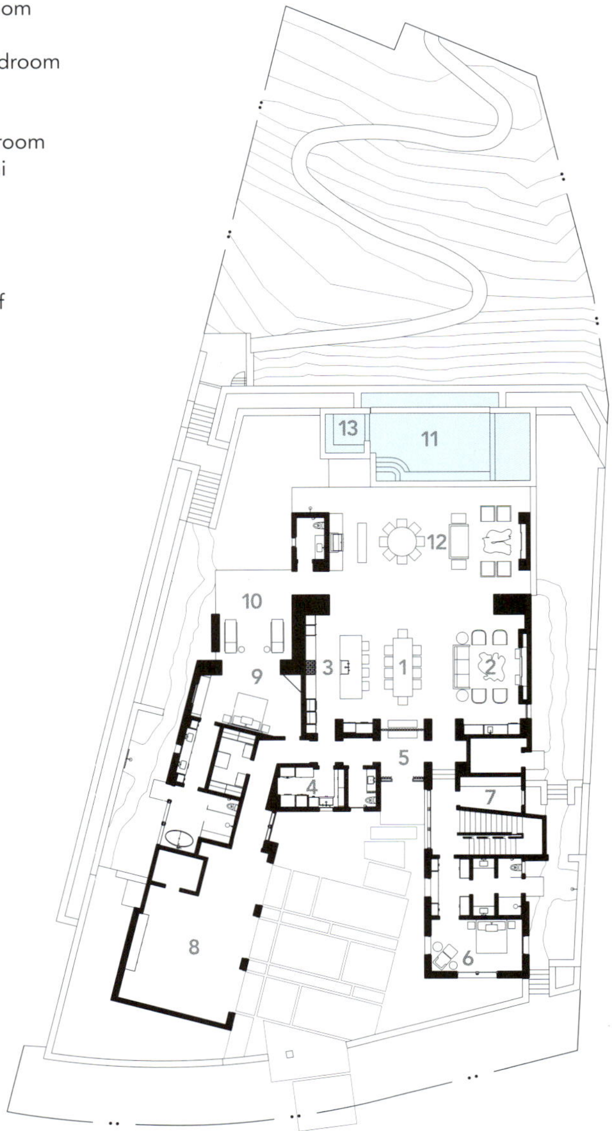

Main level floor plan

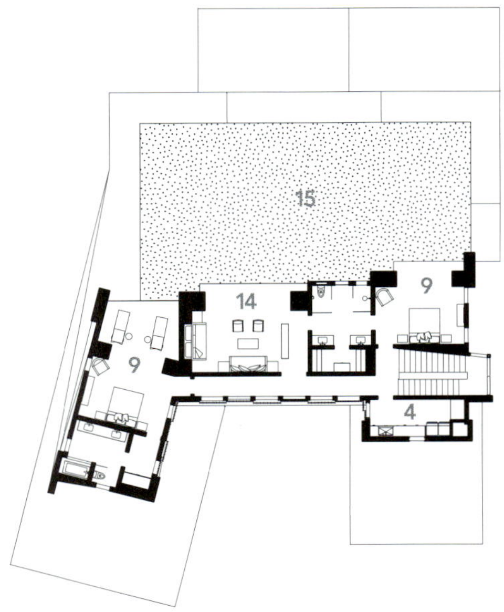

Second level floor plan

An early evening aerial view of the home

Entry door opens to a hallway with a partially screened view of the ocean, allowing the arrival experience to reveal itself slowly

The sense of aloha and tradition is created upon arrival to the home with decorative strings of carved wood leis displayed alongside a wooden bench at the entry hall. A gracious architectural atmosphere is created with warm tones of travertine floors, coral stone walls, and ohia hardwood ceilings.

Designed by Philpotts and Associates, the powder room is located just off the entry.

The casual and textured material palette of the entry flows into the main gathering area. A granite kitchen island anchors the space opposite the living area. A large ohia hardwood slab dining table has an organic free form shape that floats in the middle of the space.

Local ohia hardwood and coral stone columns set the relaxed atmosphere of the main gathering room. Interior furnishings by Philpotts and Associates.

The architecture of the main gathering space is created with coral stone columns supporting a hardwood valance wrapping the room and a hardwood ceiling floating above.

An outdoor pool shower located on the wall of the pool bath.

Interior and exterior spaces merge together when sliding doors are pulled back into wall pockets. These spaces are well sheltered from sun, wind, and rain while maintaining privacy from neighbors.

A view across the pool into the lanai and main gathering area of the home.

With ocean views, the entry hall descends a few steps to the main gathering areas.

A two-story window wall brings light to the interior in this stairway. An exterior metal brise soleil acts as a privacy screen from the adjacent neighbor.

Development restrictions required a significant setback to the second story of the home. This provided space for a green roof over the main level living spaces below, providing a garden view from the interior spaces at the second level.

A view from the bedroom lanai across the roof garden to the ocean beyond.

Four Seasons Resort O‘ahu at Ko Olina

KO OLINA, HAWAI‘I

Our firm led the design team in rebranding the former JW Marriott into the five-star Four Seasons Resort O'ahu at Ko Olina. The team repositioned the outdated hotel, designed by Edward Killingsworth in 1993, into a one-of-a-kind luxury holding for the developer and investors. While the extant hotel had a durable and expressive structure and graciously sized guest rooms, it suffered from inadequate and tired amenities, neglected finishes, and mediocre landscaping, furniture, and fixtures.

The refresh included architecture, interior design, landscape, pools, and signage and had to be delivered on a fast-track schedule for the hotelier's predetermined opening. The refresh was extensive. It called for refurbishing 358 guest accommodations (including fifty-two suites), all four restaurants, and an existing circular pool. Refurbished guest rooms strike a balance between signature Four Seasons quality and luxury Hawaiian hospitality. Banana bark wall coverings, jute-inspired carpets, and an art program produced by renowned local artists work together to form the rooms' tropical modern elegance.

The entire arrival experience, from the street through to the lobby, was enhanced. Wood detailing was added to the entry and the seventeen-story atrium to enrich the overall drama of the space and to bring a gracious elegance to the expressed and stark concrete superstructure. Tahitian-inspired ki'i, or wooden sculptures, were custom designed to greet guests upon arrival. The reception area was relocated to a discreet location to the side of the lobby with new concierge pods, replacing reception that had blocked views from the lobby to the ocean.

In addition to remodeling existing areas, we led the design of many new structures. These include a coffee lounge, two outdoor dining terraces, an adult pool with cabanas, a family pool, and spa-treatment pavilions. We removed a large lobby wall and replaced it with the Hokulea Bar. We designed the adjacent Kohola Deck, an amenity built on an existing roof, to seamlessly integrate with Killingsworth's architectural style. A new hotel wedding chapel was designed and constructed with coral stone walls and western red cedar trusses; its Arts and Crafts aesthetic draws inspiration from the architectural style of Hawaiian turn-of-the-century sensibilities. New landscaping, including the addition of a large muliwai (estuary) garden, more accurately reflects the region. Respectfully working within the bones of a Killingsworth-designed classic, we executed our vision of creating a new standard of luxury for O'ahu's first Four Seasons–branded resort.

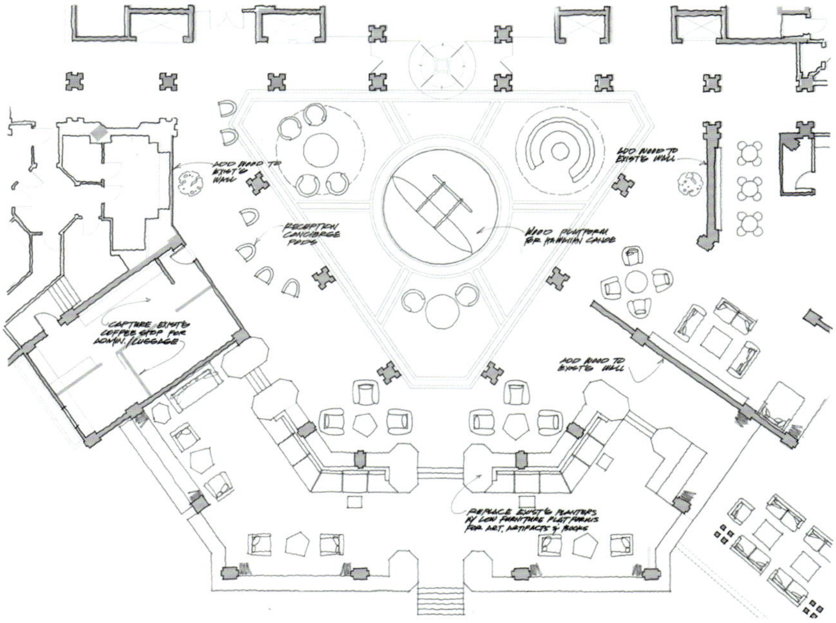

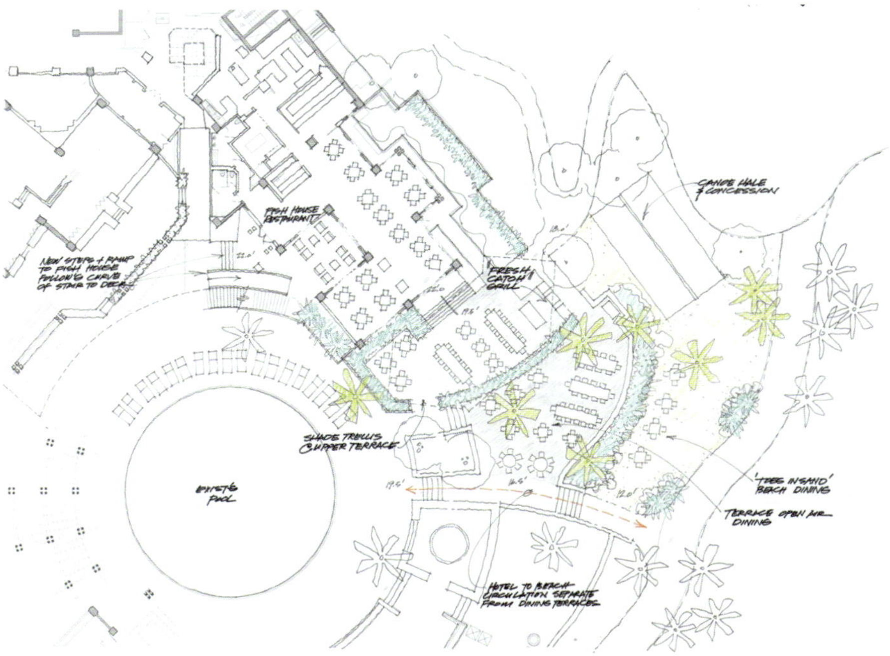

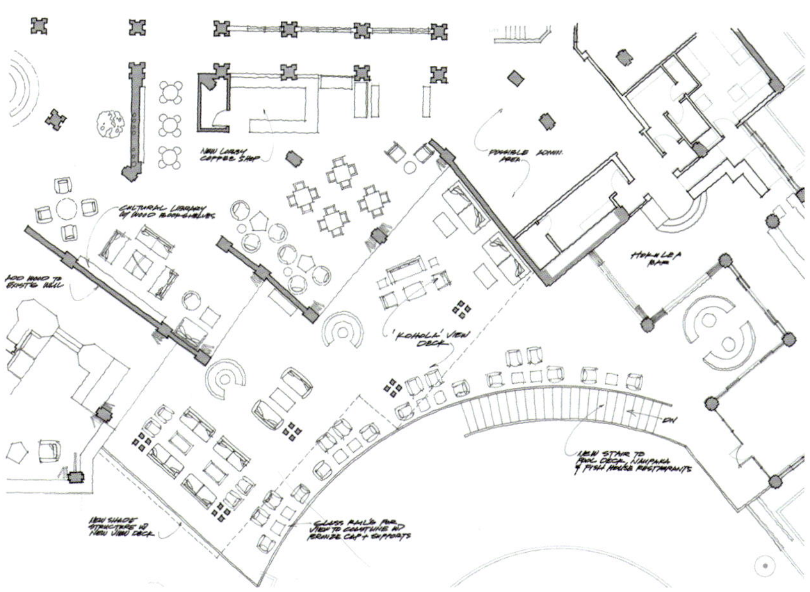

Concept studies

An intimate scale of detail and materiality was integrated into the existing structure at the arrival to raise the level of graciousness and sense of luxury. Additions include basalt stone pavers, basalt wainscot, and large teak planks for warmth behind the Four Seasons Resort signage.

A human scale and the warmth of teak wood ceiling was added to the lower tier of the dramatic terraced entry structure.

Individual concierge pods, rather than typical check-in counters, were designed for their intimate scale. Teakwood millwork panels with modernist detailing were added as backdrops to the concierge area.

Internal walls were removed to open the lobby to the ocean views, and a casual lounge and bar were designed to flow onto a new open terrace at the lobby level.

A local artisan created carved wood Polynesian ki'i, which are displayed in the center garden area of the porte cochere. These ceremonial symbols of Tahiti personify the procreative power of humankind.

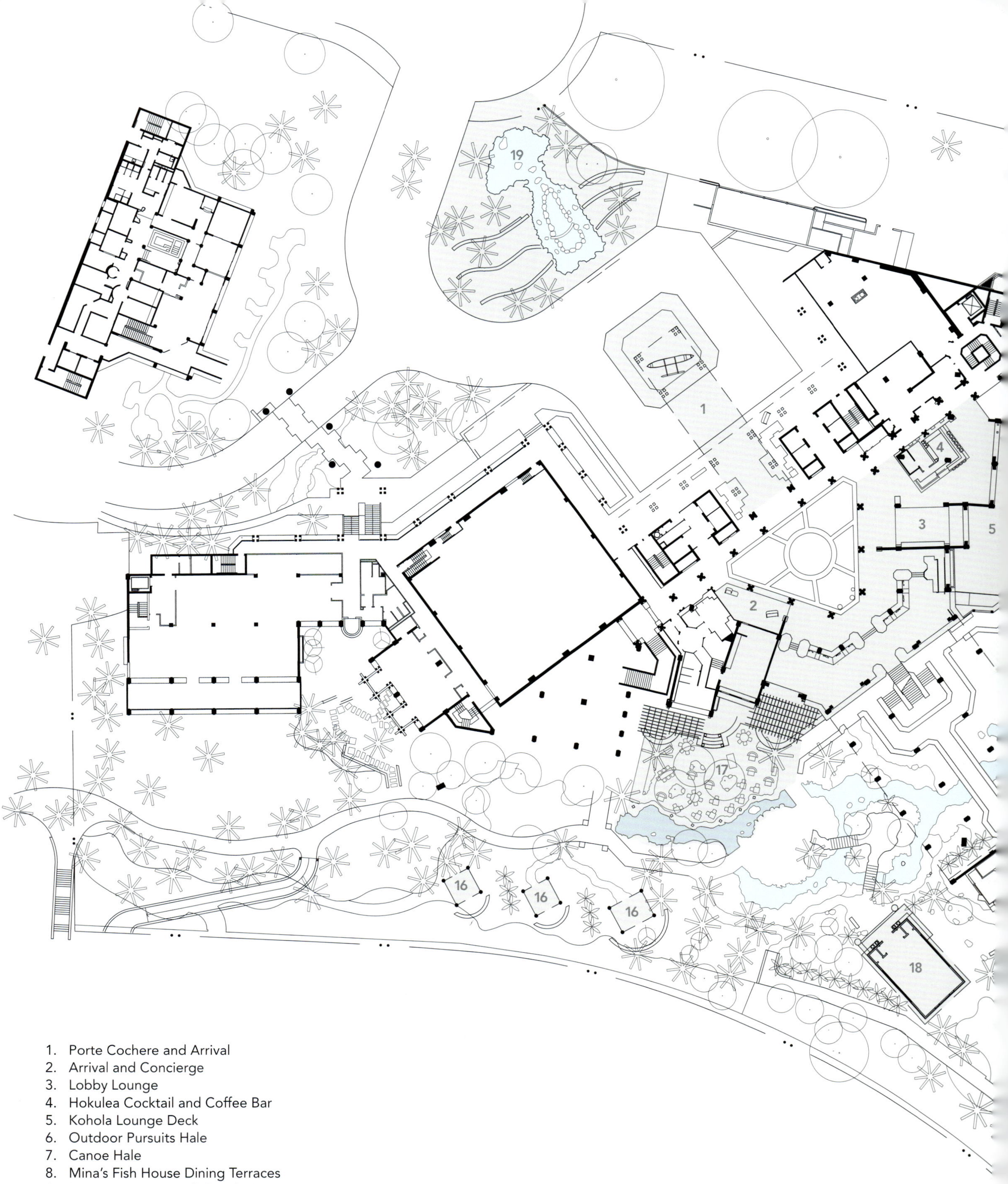

1. Porte Cochere and Arrival
2. Arrival and Concierge
3. Lobby Lounge
4. Hokulea Cocktail and Coffee Bar
5. Kohola Lounge Deck
6. Outdoor Pursuits Hale
7. Canoe Hale
8. Mina's Fish House Dining Terraces
9. Lounge Terraces with Beach Access
10. Exterior Terraces and Circular Pool
11. Waterman Pool Bar and Lounge
12. Family Pool and Spa
13. Pool Cabanas
14. Adult Pool Concierge and Restrooms
15. Adult Pool and Lounge Decks
16. Spa Treatment Pavilions
17. Noe Restaurant Dining Terrace
18. Chapel
19. Entry Water Feature and Garden

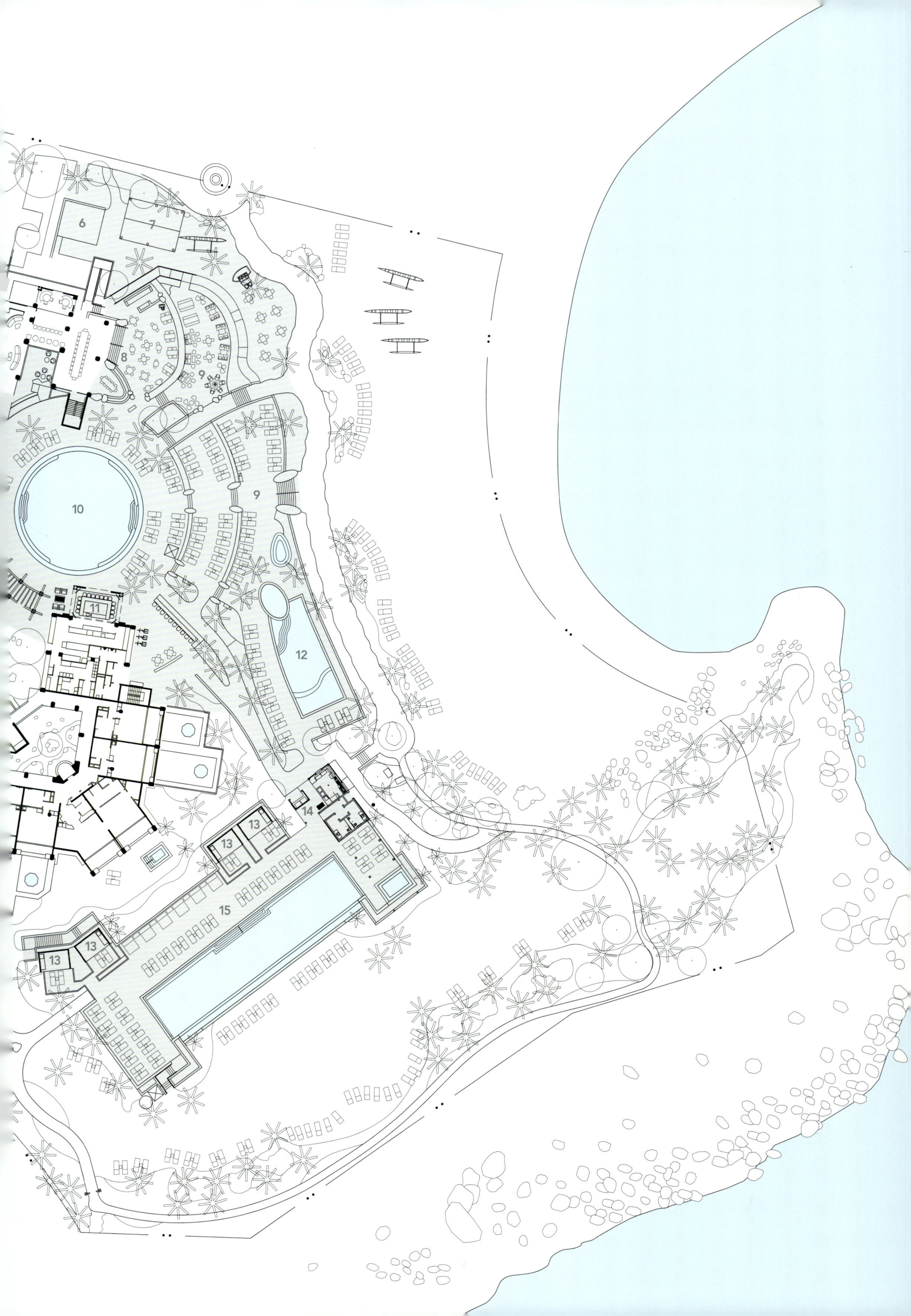

6
7
8
9
9
10
11
12
13
13
13
13
14
15

An adult pool area was positioned alongside a prime part of the coast on the hotel property. It includes a serene large pool with wrapping wood lounge decks and cabanas, a service pavilion with restrooms, and a trellis that acts as the control point to this adult zone.

A new chapel, garden, and muliwai-inspired water feature are on the north edge of the property, where they capture ocean views and respond to the adjacent parklike setting.

The chapel was inspired by humble early-twentieth-century churches built across Hawai'i by missionaries. An entry portico provides a ceremonial back drop for wedding pictures. Finish materials include wood roof shingles and coral stone masonry walls with wood millwork detailing. The modest interior architecture has white painted wood ceilings, stained wood timber trusses, and whitewashed oak benches and flooring.

The lobby lounge deck overlooking the pools, terraces, and coast.

The lobby bar and lounge are seamlessly integrated with the lobby and lanai.

The adult pool area, with its long linear pool and wrapping wood decks, was designed to provide a serene opportunity to enjoy the coastline away from the more active family areas of the property.

Mākena Beach Cottages

SOUTH MAUI, HAWAI'I

The two-story Mākena Beach Cottages sit behind Maluaka Beach along the southern edge of Discovery Land Company's 1,800-acre Mākena Golf and Beach Club property in South Maui, Hawai'i. They comprise the core of this low-density resort and were constructed within the first phase of the development, together with the club, the spa, and other residential units. They are built in a variety of contemporary and traditional designs, rather than under a narrowly prescribed style, as part of the development's vision to meld with the larger Maui community.

The design of these 3,400-square-foot cottages is a contemporary expression of early twentieth-century Hawaiian residential architecture popularized by the Honolulu-based Charles W. Dickey. The cottages are planned so each has an ocean view, a trellis-covered lanai, and a plunge pool. Side by side, double pitch hipped roofs establish their architectural scale. The exterior finishes include wood-shingled roofs, integral-color cement plaster walls, and metal-clad mahogany wood doors and windows. The interiors feature custom finishes and details befitting casual luxury.

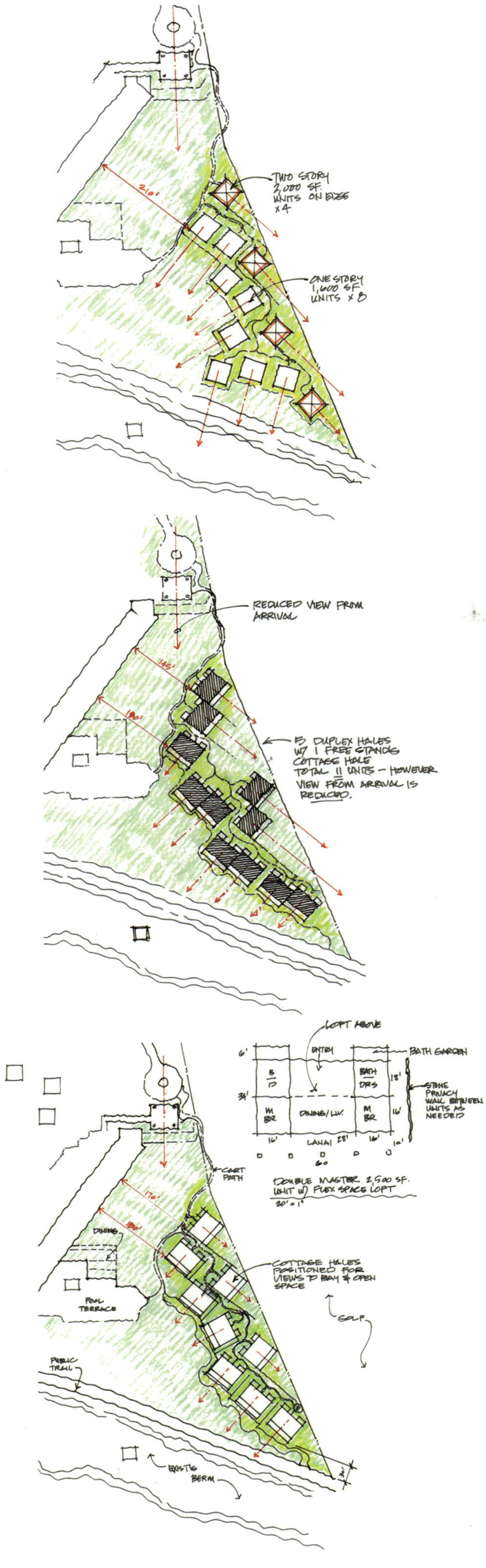

Concept design studies

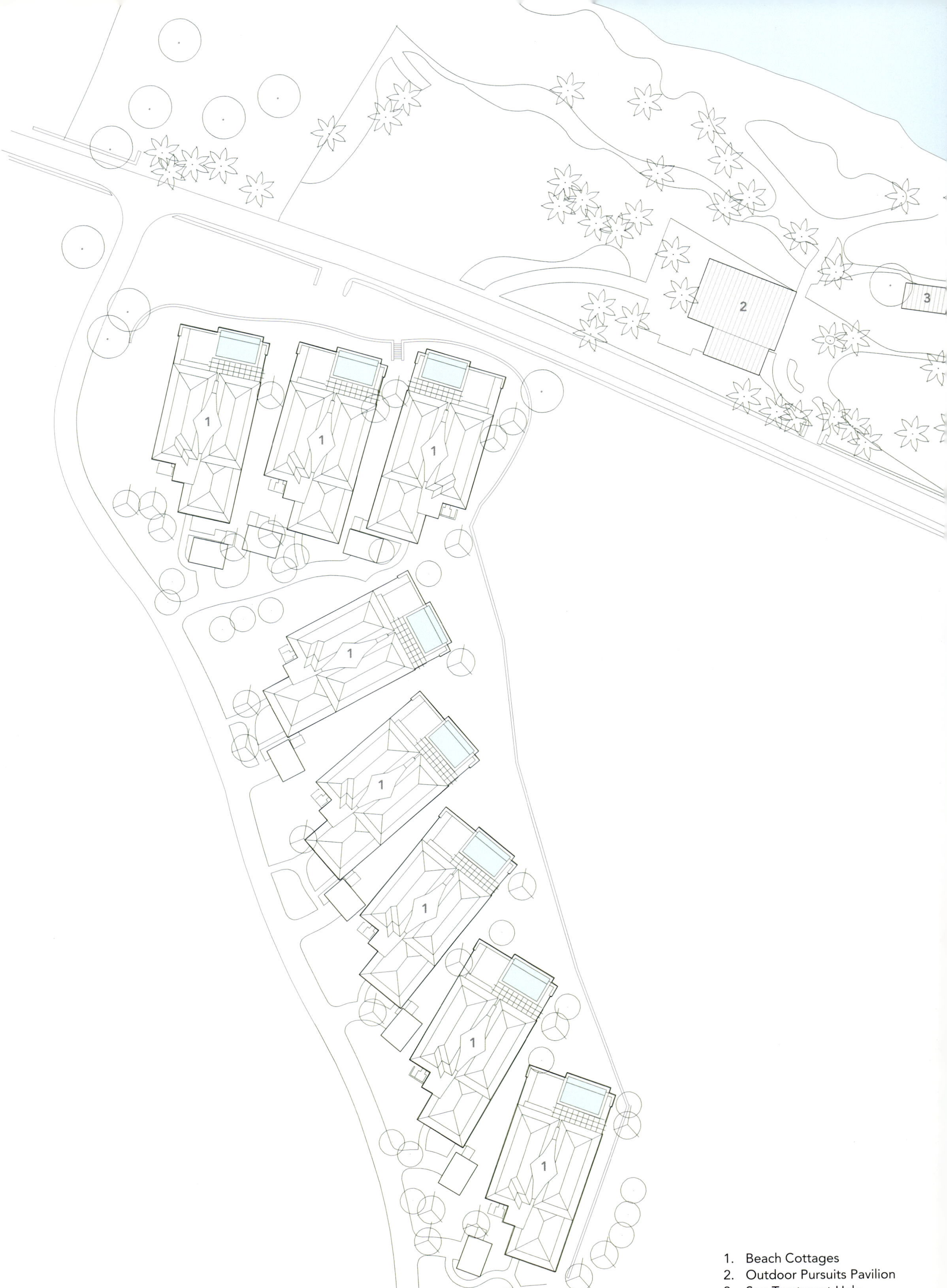

1. Beach Cottages
2. Outdoor Pursuits Pavilion
3. Spa Treatment Hale

An aerial view of the cottages.

Mauka and Makai views of the beach cottages.

Bus Stop

Mauna Kea Residence

MAUNA KEA, HAWAI‘I

Located within the venerated Mauna Kea Resort on the island of Hawai'i, the Mauna Kea Residence is tailored to the clients' desire for a contemporary tropical residence with traditional sensibilities. The home was designed in shingle style, an appropriately casual architecture for its Hawaiian setting and for family use.

Water features prominently at the residence. One arrives at the home via a bridge made of large stone slabs that cross an entry water garden and lead to the front door and into the main gathering area. On the opposite side of the home, a swimming pool brings water alongside living spaces. The pool is designed for both its cooling effect and its aesthetic impact, as it refracts and reflects light about the interior.

The living spaces open to a sweeping view of the north Kohala coast through large, pocketed glass doors. These doors merge interior spaces to this view as well as the gardens and the larger tropical setting. The clients' program for the residence included an entry, main gathering area with lanai, separate dining room, outdoor kitchen with barbecue, family/recreation room, office, primary suite with sitting area, his and hers dressing areas and bath with outdoor shower garden, four guest bedroom suites, a swimming pool and spa, and solar-powered hot water. They also asked for a widow's walk to be included in the design of their home. We incorporated this idea of a roof-high vantage point as a cupola on top of an outdoor pavilion.

Natural finish materials contribute to the architectural quality and to the home's durability. Exterior materials consist of low-profile flat clay tile roof shingles, walls of driftwood gray cedar shingles, integral-color cement plaster, and textured coral stone. Interior materials include travertine stone floors, cherry wood cabinetry and trim, and marble and granite counters.

Concept elevation

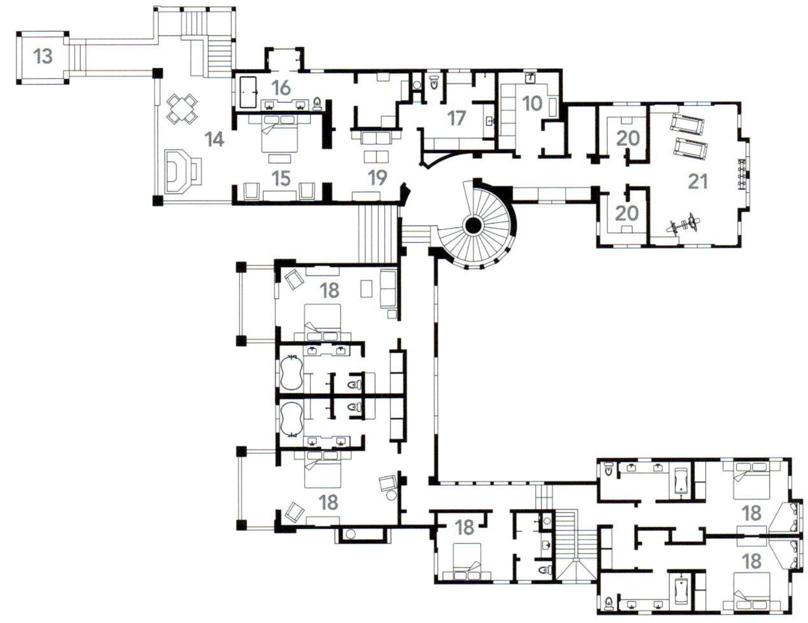

Main level floor plan

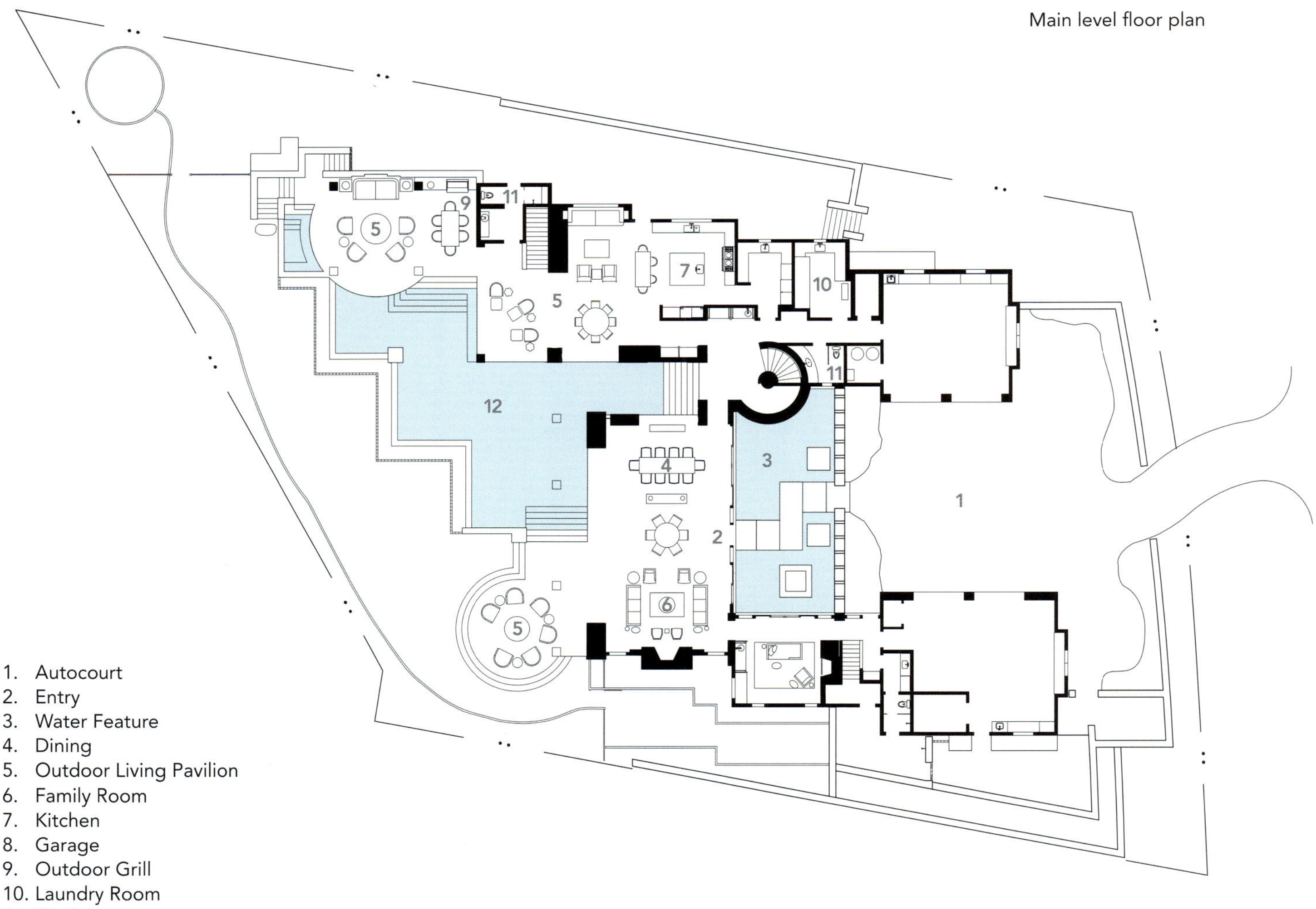

Second level floor plan

1. Autocourt
2. Entry
3. Water Feature
4. Dining
5. Outdoor Living Pavilion
6. Family Room
7. Kitchen
8. Garage
9. Outdoor Grill
10. Laundry Room
11. Washroom
12. Pool
13. Widow's Walk
14. Lanai
15. Primary Bedroom
16. Primary Bathroom
17. Primary Bathroom
18. Guest Bedroom
19. Sitting Room
20. Office
21. Exercise Room

A view of the arrival gate into the entry water garden.

The neighborhood view.

A small widow's walk above the lanai/pool pavilion is accessed from the second level.

Philpotts and Associates curated an eclectic mix of new furnishings and owner-furnished artifacts into an elegant Hawaiian Asian design.

A night view of the entry water garden.

Previous page: The poolside lanai provides sheltered outdoor living and captures views across the hillside community and to the ocean beyond.

The client is a chef and TV personality. Her request for an open kitchen with casual dining and living in the same room reflects her passions and how her life revolves around her interests.

A backlit onyx stone fireplace anchors one end of the main gathering room.

Bedrooms, including the prime bedroom above, are on the second level. Their eclectic interior furnishings are Hawaiian and ocean oriented.

The interior designer selected hues of pink and blue, favorite colors of the family's daughters, for their compatibility with the cherry wood millwork and hardwood floors. The interiors are tied into the shingle style of the home.

An elliptical window provides a view from the stair lobby at the second level to the ocean.

On the boards and unbuilt works

Mākena Golf and Beach Club

SOUTH MAUI, HAWAI'I

A Discovery Land Company community, Mākena Golf and Beach Club is a members-only resort community on South Maui. A community-based development vision of sustainability guides the project, and our firm is the lead architect for more than 490,000 square feet of club amenities and residential dwellings comprising the 24-acre core of this 1,800-acre development. The initial phase within this core consists of a 64,821-square-foot club, a 17,812-square-foot spa, the beach bar and outdoor pursuits; six 22,481-square-foot club residences; ten 3,648-square-foot beach cottages, ten 67,250-square-foot Molokini residences, the eight-unit 27,886-square-foot Hale Kehau, and the thirty-unit 176,215-square-foot multifamily Kula Villas.

The architectural design of the club is attentive to the spatial order and circulation within users' experiences, from arrival, to within the club, to the gardens and pools. This objective plays out in merging exterior and interior spaces and in the efficient operations of the club. The club amenity spaces and concierge offices are located on the main level, with back of house functions and parking on the basement level, and club residential dwellings on the second level.

The club is conceived as a garden courtyard building, a type that has proven to be well adapted to tropical climates, as natural ventilation allows a building to breathe. Amenity spaces and residences above are organized around a water garden that functions as a transitional space for arrival and departure. Stone walls wrap the courtyard at the club level, and a wood screen wraps the open-air walkway to the residences. Large doors open the bar and dining spaces to the lanais and views. The interior architecture and design have modernist sensibilities, while their textures and materials reference the club's Polynesian location. The bar and dining spaces are designed for conviviality befitting casual use by family and friends.

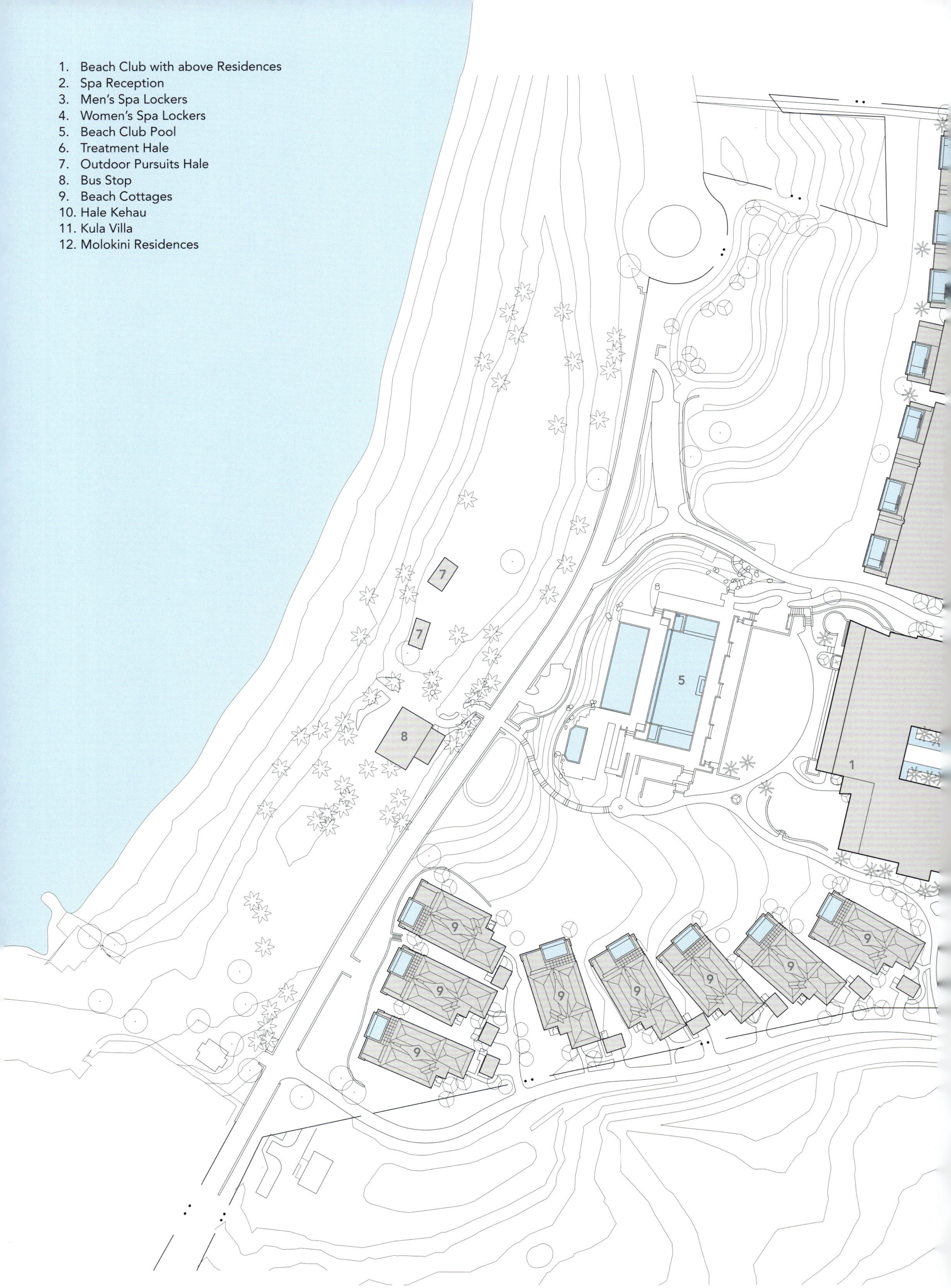
1. Beach Club with above Residences
2. Spa Reception
3. Men's Spa Lockers
4. Women's Spa Lockers
5. Beach Club Pool
6. Treatment Hale
7. Outdoor Pursuits Hale
8. Bus Stop
9. Beach Cottages
10. Hale Kehau
11. Kula Villa
12. Molokini Residences
7
7
8
5
1
9

12
11
10
9
9
11
11
10
11
11
2
4
6
6
6
6

Mākena Molokini Residences

SOUTH MAUI, HAWAI'I

With ocean views to Lana'i, Molokini Crater, and Kaho'olawe, the Mākena Molokini Residences extend the restrained tropical modern nature of the adjacent Mākena Golf and Beach Club (shown on the previous pages). These units incorporate low-slope roofs that open toward the ocean to minimize their impact on the views of residential units behind them. The interior living, dining, and kitchen areas of these five-bedroom residences are free of structural walls and columns; their post-tensioned concrete floors allow large expanses of floor space. Large glass doors open the living and bedroom spaces to the views, large lanais, and the pool garden at the lower level.

Exterior finishes include coral-colored plaster walls; cedar soffits, wall panels, and trim; and cleft basalt walls. Dark bronze aluminum doors, windows, and louver screens provide sun control and privacy.

North Shore Residence

WEST MAUI, HAWAI'I

The site for this residence commands spectacular views of the dramatic mountains of West Maui. Stretched across a gently sloping hillside within a twenty-seven-acre farm, this residence is a direct response to its setting. Its spatially fluid interiors and large glass floor-to-ceiling windows and doors capture mountain and ocean views from three sides, while it presents a less permeable facade toward the prevailing winds from the northeast. The home is a series of spaces and experiences organized around a garden courtyard proportioned to the golden section. A breezeway wraps the courtyard and connects the main gathering spaces to the bedrooms and the garage.

The tropical modern architecture has low-slope roofs that open interior spaces to the exterior and views. Large eaves protect the interior from sun and rain. A second-story main bedroom cantilevers dramatically over a lanai and toward West Maui.

Building materials were selected for their connection to the island, their durability, and their contribution to the residence's restrained aesthetic and refined character. Interior spaces are influenced by the exterior material palette. These spaces include rift-sawed white oak doors and trim; light gray, wide plank oak floors; blackened steel accents; and large basalt columns.

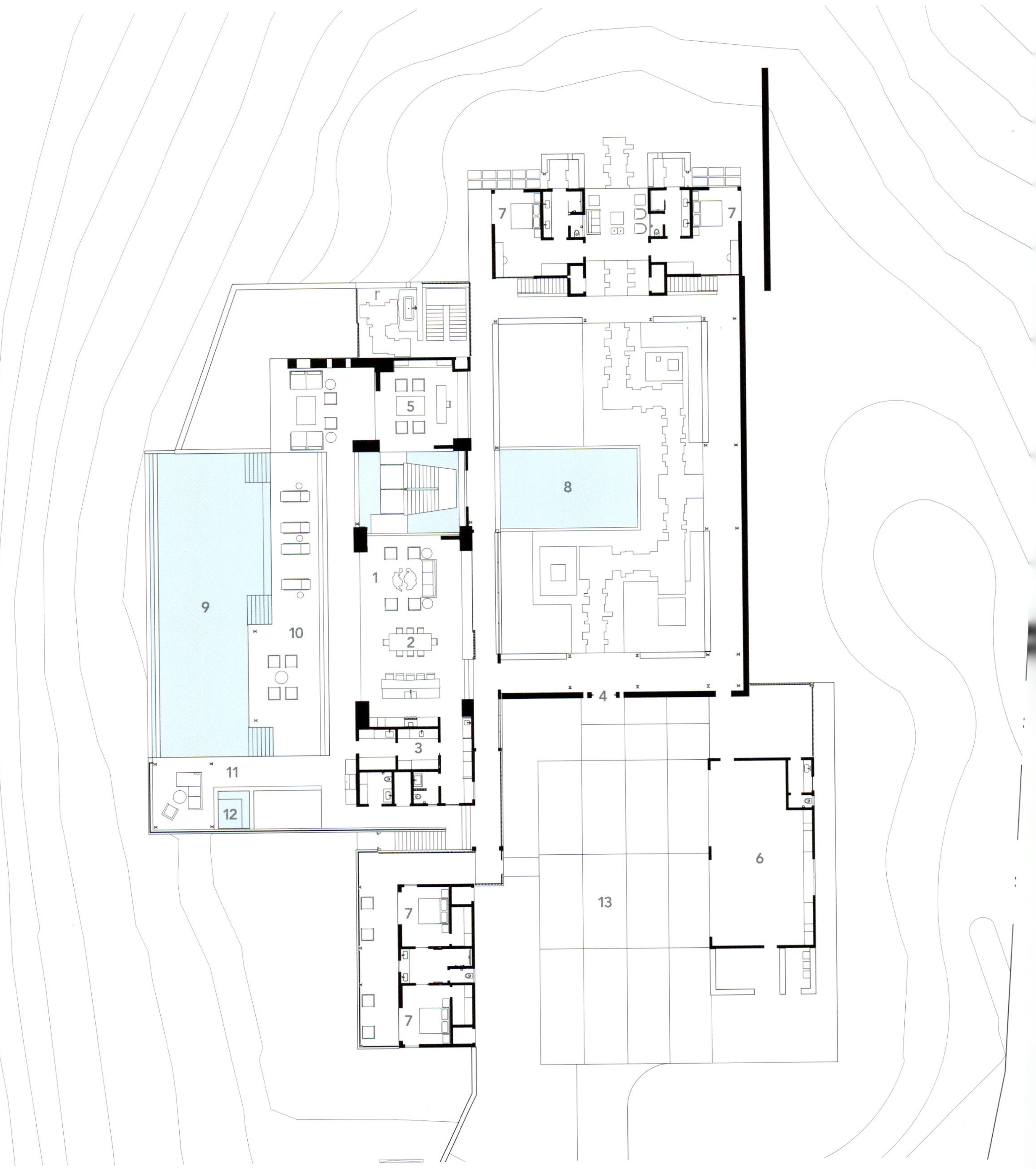

1. Main Gathering
2. Dining
3. Laundry Room
4. Entry
5. Office
6. Garage
7. Guest Suite
8. Water Feature
9. Pool
10. Pool Terrace
11. Pool Pavilion
12. Spa
13. Autocourt

Chileno Hillside Villas

LOS CABOS, MEXICO

Alongside Mexico's Sea of Cortez, Chileno Bay Golf and Beach Club is a members-only 1,200-acre residential community in the Los Cabos corridor. Chileno Hillside Residences reside on a twelve-acre coastal site within the master planned community.

The architectural design reflects Mexico's embrace of modernism and creates a contextually responsive architecture befitting place, climate, and buyer tastes. The Los Cabos region has experienced much growth with luxury resort development, resulting in a wide range of exciting modern and contemporary architecture mixed with more traditional styles.

Our firm provided architectural design for the development's first phase, consisting of thirty-four residences within thirteen buildings, ranging in size from 2,350 to 4,991 square feet. Thirteen multistory, multiunit buildings are stepped and integrated into the steep hillsides. The undulating topography necessitated that each building adjust to the terrain; this offered an opportunity to individualize the buildings, the terraces, and the residences.

The minimal architecture is harmonious with the arid climate, the stark hillsides, and the rugged coastline. The exterior finish materials were selected to enhance the modern character. Taking cues from the simple, elegant, romantic appearance of the white plaster hillside villages along the Amalfi Coast, we used just a few subtle off-white plaster colors together with local stone as the restrained palette of the buildings' exteriors.

Each residence has a private courtyard entrance, a golf cart garage, and its own terrace and pool. Interior gathering areas open to terraces and views through tall, pocketed, sliding glass doors.

Small cobblestone roadways meander with the topography, while hillside stairs are woven together with stone terracing to provide access throughout the community. Evocative of hillside villages of Amalfi that were built over time and feel of the land, Chileno Hillside Villas has buildings, roads, stairs, and gardens that are highly integrated with the hillsides—designed as one holistic concept.

Papagayo Residence

PAPAGAYO, COSTA RICA

The design of this two-story residence was conceived as a treehouse where one could live among the tree canopy, birds, and wildlife. The home was sited for minimal ecological disturbance on a small, wooded jungle hilltop within a resort development along Costa Rica's Gulf of Papagayo.

This 6,500-square-foot residence is essentially a timber structure that has an open floor plan, with common gathering areas on the upper level and bedrooms on the lower level. The open timber structure is expressed with glazing between, and large glass doors open interior spaces to the tree canopy, jungle, and ocean views.

Local materials such as tropical hardwoods and stone connect the home to the site and environment. Material colorations were selected to harmonize with the natural environment.

Sawtooth Residence

IDAHO

On a twenty-six-acre site in the Rocky Mountains, a river skirts the northern reaches of the property where this home is situated. The land is considered an ecotone, a region of transition between two biological communities. Wildlife is often prevalent in an ecotone, and eagles, hawks, ospreys, elk, deer, fox, muskrat, beaver, rabbits and weasels are plentiful. Aspen, Cottonwood trees and willows dominate the river valley reaches; Doug Fir, Spruce, and Pine trees populate the mountain sides.

The home has been designed with a contemporary mountain character inspired from local ranch vernacular. With the sensibilities of a ranch, the home is organized as a series of connected building forms arranged around an arrival court that orients to the south to bring sunlight to the interior spaces.

Gable roofs cover the interconnected buildings and a simple palette of exterior materials consists of patinated grey metal roof, recycled barnwood, and stone exterior walls with metal clad wood windows. Primary living and entertaining spaces have large interior volumes to better enjoy views to the surrounding mountains. Interior spaces are being designed for the owner's contemporary art collection. A barn with a second story accessory dwelling has been completed as the first phase of the home.

Firm Profile

Established in 2005, de Reus Architects' approach to design is based on collaboration, working with each client and circumstance to reveal the nature of place and find an individual expression for each project. The firm leverages the relationship between place and building to create lasting memories for future generations. Nature, craft, and design—luxury defined.

A full-service firm with studios in Sun Valley, Idaho, and Waimea and Wailea, Hawai'i, de Reus Architects specializes in the design and planning of distinctive residential, resort, and hospitality projects across North America. Dedicated to design excellence, the firm has won numerous awards from the American Institute of Architects and has been featured in hundreds of publications, including the *New York Times, Architectural Digest, Dezeen,* and *Mountain Living.* In 2010, *Architectural Digest* included Mark de Reus in its AD100, a listing of the world's top designers and architects.

Leadership

Mark de Reus

Mark de Reus, founding partner of de Reus Architects, is widely known for his site-sensitive and highly crafted architecture that is intimately tied to location, culture, and client. For more than forty years, Mark has helped clients realize their visions across a diverse range of projects, including the planning and design of high-end residences, multifaceted resorts and hotels, spas, retail establishments, and wineries.

In 2010, *Architectural Digest* named Mark to the AD100, a listing of the world's top hundred architects and designers. Mark's work has been recognized through numerous design awards and featured in dozens of publications, including the *New York Times*, *Architectural Digest*, *Dezeen*, *Sun Valley*, *Western Home Journal*, *Tatler Asia*, *Mountain Living*, *Cocotraie*, *Modern Luxury Hawaii*, and *Ocean Home*. Mark's work has been the subject of two books, *Tropical Experience* and *Sanctuary*, both published by ORO Editions. In 2008, HGTV featured his design of the Seaside Hale Residence as part of the program "Amazing Waterfront Homes."

Prior to starting his own firm, Mark held various leadership roles at notable practices, including design principal at Hart Howerton's Hawai'i office, director at the Jakarta, Indonesia-based architecture firm PAI, and senior vice president at San Francisco–based BAR Architects. Mark holds a Bachelor of Architecture degree from the University of Idaho, where he has served on the Dean's Advisory Council for the College of Art and Architecture.

Dan Dzakowic

Over the span of twenty years, Dan has led the design of dozens of private residences and resort developments throughout the world, with a particular focus on projects in North America and Oceania. Dan joined de Reus Architects in 2005 and became an associate in 2012 and a partner in 2021.

His expertise in planning, design, and management has been central to maintaining the firm's reputation for project delivery.

His experience includes the management of large, complex projects such as the Four Seasons Resort O'ahu at Ko Olina, a ten-acre, five-hundred-room destination resort hotel. His design approach teases out the nuances of his clients' aspirations, merging them in a contextual response the sites in which he works. Dan serves as studio director of the firm's Hawai'i office, where he leads business development and the imagining of new projects at all scales. Dan's current and recent work includes numerous private residences, a private resort villa in Sayulita, Mexico, and the thirty-four-unit Chileno Hillside Villas development for Discovery Land Company in Puerto Vallarta, Mexico.

A graduate of University of Hawai'i at Mānoa's School of Architecture, Dan is a licensed architect in the states of Hawai'i and Nevada, a member of the American Institute of Architects, and a US Green Building Council accredited LEED AP professional.

John Rowland

John has more than twenty-four years of experience leading residential and commercial projects, including the notable Mākena Golf and Beach Club. Joining the firm in 2005, John was named a senior associate in 2015. He is a consummate team leader, particularly effective at keeping the larger design issues in focus while coordinating project teams. He is skilled at maintaining the integrity of his work, ensuring architectural details meet or exceed established project parameters.

John has been involved in many of the firm's most recognized projects, including the Ka'upulehu Beach Club, the Kuki'o Golf Club, and numerous significant private residences. Prior to joining de Reus Architects in 2005, John worked for several firms in Boise, Idaho, both large and small, as well as leading his own firm. John holds a Master of Architecture degree and a Bachelor of Architecture degree from the University of Idaho.

Christopher Strahle

Christopher Strahle began his career at de Reus Architects as an intern in 2008 and was made an associate with the firm in 2017. While Chris has worked on a vast array of project types, his focus is on high-end residences and resorts in various locations ranging from high mountain deserts to tropical seasides. He values design that celebrates the connection between built structures and their surroundings and has a strong interest and sensitivity to site-specific context, materiality, light, and experience.

Prior to returning to de Reus Architects in 2012, he completed his doctoral practicum in New York City while working as a designer at Kohn Pedersen Fox and volunteering with New York Urban Green. He also assisted in the expansion to the Dallas World Aquarium in Dallas, Texas.

Christopher holds a Doctorate in Architecture from the University of Hawai'i at Mānoa, where he studied tropical regionalism and environmental design and served as a sustainability adviser for fellow students while working as an assistant professor at the School of Architecture.

Louis Kauffman

With more than thirty-five years of professional experience, Louis has designed a wide range of projects, from bespoke private residences and ranches to numerous cultural, large-scale commercial, and institutional projects. A principal in de Reus Architects, he is engaged in all facets of the practice, including design, management, and business development.

Eschewing a form-based approach to design, Louis sees architecture as an experience marrying the visible and invisible qualities of the land to carry the story of clients and their site. His expertise with large-scale projects has focused on translating the experience of place through intimacy of scale and kinesthetic responses to space. The resultant body of work is noted for the timeless character of its design, emphasizing clarity of purpose, meticulous craftsmanship, and quiet poetry.

Over the course of his career, Louis has worked for noted firms including Hammel, Green and Abrahamson; Skidmore Owings & Merrill; and Altoon + Porter, where he served as studio director for their Amsterdam office. Louis holds a Master of Architecture degree from Harvard University and Bachelor of Arts degree from UCLA.

Projects Credits

KAUHALE KAI RESIDENCE

Project Team
Mark de Reus, Design Principal
Stephen Ewing, Principal
Ian Glass, Jason Alden, Project Managers
Dan Dzakowic, John Rowland, Lindsey Akiona
Project Consultants
St. Dizier Design, Interior Design for furnishings
David Tamura, Landscape Architect
GFDS, Structural Engineer
Prepose Engineering System, Inc., Mechanical Engineer
KGM, Architectural Lighting
Lighting and Engineering Integrated, Inc, Electrical Engineer
Joe Fletcher, Photography

BIAS RESIDENCE

Project Team
Mark de Reus, Design Principal
Eric Anderson, Project Manager
Ian Glass, Christopher Strahle
Project Consultants
Philpotts and Associates, Interior Furnishings
David Tamura, Landscape Architect
Kahiau Design Group, Structural Engineer
Matthew Millman, Photography

YELLOW JACKET

Project Team
Mark de Reus, Design Principal
John Rowland, Project Manager
Mark Thompson
Project Consultants
Dennis E. Zirbel, Architect of Record
St. Dizier Design, Interior Design
Ed Haag, Landscape Architect
Greenwood Homes, Builder
Gabe Border, Photography

BIG WOOD RESIDENCE

Project Team
Mark de Reus, Design Principal
John Rowland, Project Manager
Christopher Strahle, Lindsey Akiona,
Josh Melling, Dylan Snelling
Project Consultants
Sequoia Contract Works, Interior Furnishings
NS Consulting, Landscape Architect
Maxwell Engineering, Structural Engineer
KGM Architectural Lighting
Young Construction, Builder
Gabe Border, Photography

ANCIENT PONDS RESIDENCE

Project Team
Mark de Reus, Design Principal
Dan Dzakowic, Project Manager
Lindsey Akiona, Miliana Johnson
Project Consultants
Philpotts and Associates, Interior Design
David Tamura, Landscape Architect
GFDS Engineers, Structural Engineer
KGM, Architectural Lighting
Joe Fletcher, Photography

MAUNA KEA RESIDENCE

Project Team
Mark de Reus, Design Principal
Stephen Ewing, Design and Managing Principal
John Rowland, Project Manager
Ian Glass, Mark Thompson, Eric Tiles, Dan Dzakowic,
Lindsey Akiona
Project Consultants
Philpotts and Associates, Interior Design
GFDS, Structural Engineer
Lighting and Engineering Integrated, Inc, Electrical Engineer
Greg Boyer, Landscape Architect
Kevin Roach, Builder
Roger Wade, Photography

TROPICAL RESIDENCE

Project Team
Mark de Reus, Design Principal
Dan Dzakowic, Project Manager
Christopher Strahle, Brandt Loo, Lindsey Akiona
Project Consultants
Philpotts and Associates, Interior Design
David Tamura, Landscape Architect
Kahiau Design Group, Structural Engineer
KDG Hawaii, Todd Dwight, Structural Engineer
KGM, Architectural Lighting
Ethan Tweedie, Photography

FOUR SEASONS RESORT O'AHU AT KO OLINA

Project Team
Mark de Reus, Design Principal
Dan Dzakowic, Project Manager

Christopher Strahle, Brandt Loo, John Rowland, Matt Youdall
Project Consultants
G70, Architect of Record
Philpotts and Associates, Interior Design
PBR, Landscape Architect
Christian Horan Photography; Andrea Brizzi Photography

MĀKENA BEACH COTTAGES

Project Team
Mark de Reus, Design Principal
John Rowland, Project Manager
Mark Thompson, Christopher Strahle, Ian Glass
Project Consultants
Discovery Design, Interior Design
WCIT Architecture, Architect of Record
VITA Planning and Landscape Architecture, Landscape Architect
Discovery Builders, Builder
Travis Rowan, Photography

CORAL HOUSE

Project Team
Mark de Reus, Design Principal
Eric Anderson, Project Architect
Dan Dzakowic, Christopher Strahle, Lindsey Akiona
Project Consultants
Philpotts and Associates, Interior Design
Kahiau Design Group, Structural Engineer
Vita Planning and Landscape Architecture, Landscape Architect
Maui Mechanical, Mechanical Engineering
Colt Construction, Builder
Travis Rowan, Photography

PUNTA SAYULITA CLUB AND TREEHOUSE

Project Team
Mark de Reus, Design Principal
Stephen Ewing, Design Principal (Treehouse)
Jason Alden, Project Manager
Christopher Strahle, Lindsey Akiona, Ian Glass,
Gordon Karau, Hector Troncoso
Developer
Contact Development
Brett Ellsworth, Partner
Kevin Roberts, Partner
Project Consultants
Rachel Horn Interiors, Furnishings for Club, Casita, Casa Villas
Hannah Waxman Interiors, Furnishings for Treehouse
Vita Planning and Landscape Architecture, Landscape Architect
Petr Myska, Photography

MĀKENA GOLF AND BEACH CLUB

Project Team
Mark de Reus, Design Principal
John Rowland, Project Manager
Matt Youdall, Mark Thompson, Christopher Strahle,
Josh Melling, Spencer Woodard
Project Consultants
FDG Group, Interior Design
Tipping Structural, Structural Engineering
SSFM, Civil Engineering
VITA, Planning and Landscape Architecture
Kolohe Design, Pools & Water Features
Lighting Design Alliance, Lighting

MĀKENA MOLOKINI RESIDENCES

Project Team
Mark de Reus, Design Principal
John Rowland, Project Manager
Mark Thompson, Spencer Woodard
Project Consultants
VITA, Planning and Landscape Architecture
Tipping Structural, Structural Engineering
Kolohe Design, Pools & Water Features
Lighting Design Alliance, Lighting

NORTH SHORE RESIDENCE

Project Team
Mark de Reus, Design Principal
Christopher Strahle, Project Manager
Ashley Fassbender, Josh Melling
Project Consultants
Kahiau Design Group, Structural Engineer
Maui Mechanical, Mechanical Engineering
Pono Building Co, Builder

CHILENO HILLSIDE VILLAS

Project Team
Mark de Reus, Design Principal
Dan Dzakowic, Project Manager
AJ Taaca, Dylan Snelling, Christopher Strahle, Josh Melling
Project Consultants
Discovery Design, Interior Design
VITA, Planning and Landscape Architecture

PAPAGAYO RESIDENCE

Project Team
Mark de Reus, Design Principal
JJ Rumpeltes, Ian Glass

Book Credits

Introduction by Joseph Giovannini

Joseph Giovannini heads Giovannini Associates, a design firm based in New York and Los Angeles. He holds a Master of Architecture degree from Harvard's Graduate School of Design. He has taught advanced and graduate studios at Columbia University Graduate School of Architecture, UCLAs Graduate School of Architecture and Urban Planning, the University of Southern Californias School of Architecture, and at the University of Innsbruck. His projects have ranged from the adaptive reuse of a large trucking facility into lofts to house additions and apartment interiors. A graduate of Yale University, where he did his B.A. in English, he also holds a Master of Arts degree in French Language and Literature from La Sorbonne, Paris, Middlebury College Program. Besides heading his design practice, Mr. Giovannini has written on architecture and design for three decades for such publications as the *New York Times, Architectural Record, Art in America, Art Forum* and *Architecture Magazine.* He has also served as the architecture critic for *New York Magazine* and the *Los Angeles Herald Examiner.* Published design projects have appeared in *Architectural Digest,* the *Los Angeles Times Magazine,* the *New York Times, A + U, Domus, House and Garden, GA Houses, Architekur und Wohnen, Sites,* and *Interior Design.* He lives in New York with his wife, Christine Pittel, and daughter Isabella.

Edited and designed by Pablo Mandel

Pablo Mandel is an Argentine-Canadian book designer and editor. For more than two decades he has built a career designing books on architecture, working with renowned architects, universities, musicians, and artists around the world. Pablo is the founder of Circular Studio, a collaborative graphic design practice with focus on brand identity for architects. He is also an associate art director for ORO Editions. He is co-editor of *France Sketchbooks*, with Laurie Olin. Born in Argentina in 1970, Pablo graduated from Buenos Aires University in 1995 with a degree in graphic design and emigrated to Canada shortly after. He is a professional member of the Society of Graphic Designers of Canada (www.gdc.net). His book designs have been published internationally and have been the recipient of numerous awards. In parallel to his graphic design activity, Pablo has been active for more than twenty years as a member of the League of Crafty Guitarists and Guitar Circles. Last but not least: Pablo is an artist, a husband, and a father.

Acknowledgments

de Reus Architects book team

Mark de Reus
Christopher Strahle
Joshua Melling
Carson Johnston
Emily Lizarraga

Nature Photography

Front matter, pages 4–15:
James Bourret
David Stoecklein
Nick Price
Christian Horan
Eric Piasecki
Jim Kruger

Back matter, pages 348–359:
Ethan Tweedie
Erik Tollefsrud
Pete Piriya
David Stoecklein
James Bourret
Nick Price

The projects featured in this book have all been completed since our first book, *Tropical Experience,* was released in 2011. They couldn't have been accomplished without our clients' trust in our abilities and understanding as we sought to realize their visions. We appreciate their mixture of patience, faith, nurturing, and good humor as we worked together to develop the best ideas.

We've worked with many talented and dedicated individuals who've contributed to these projects and have tried to identify them in the credits section. My apologies if we missed anyone. I extend my appreciation to my partner, Dan Dzakowic, as well as to John Rowland, Christopher Strahle, and Josh Melling. This book would not have been possible without their support and contributions.

I owe special thanks to our guest author, Joseph Giovannini, for his insightful essay about our practice and the wonderful profession of architecture. Additionally, I offer my thanks to Will Kitchens, who edited my Foreword on the rituals of practice.

Creating this book was a rewarding experience, guided by the estimable Gordon Goff, managing director of ORO Editions, and the talented book designer, Pablo Mandel.

Many fine photographers contributed their artistic work, and Jeff Brink developed the computer-generated illustrations.

I'm most grateful to my wife, Lizzie, for her understanding and love.

— Mark de Reus

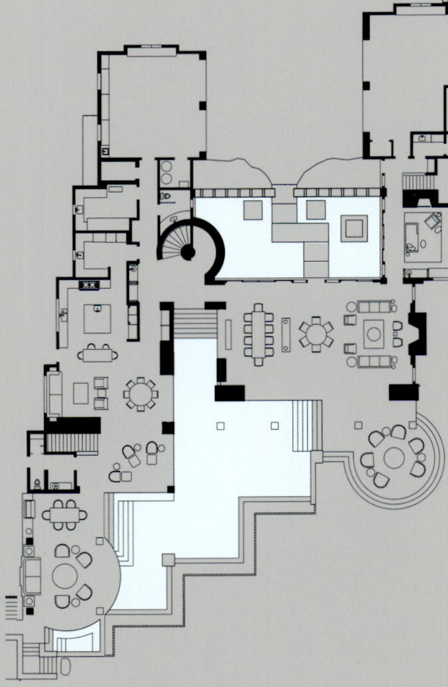
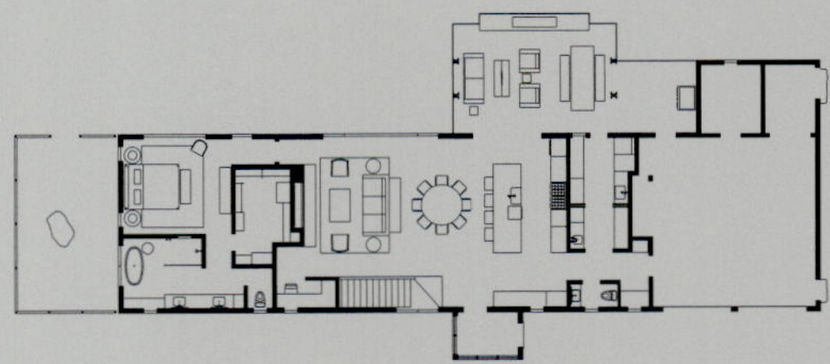

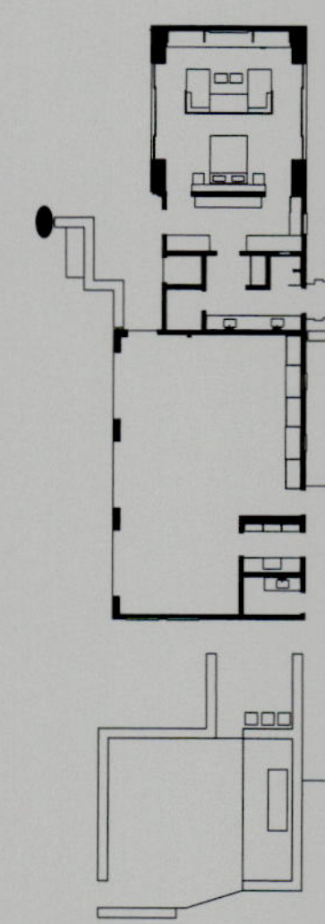
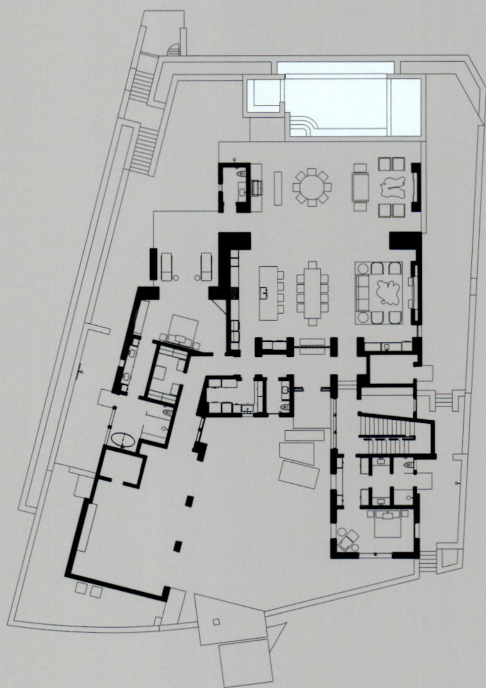

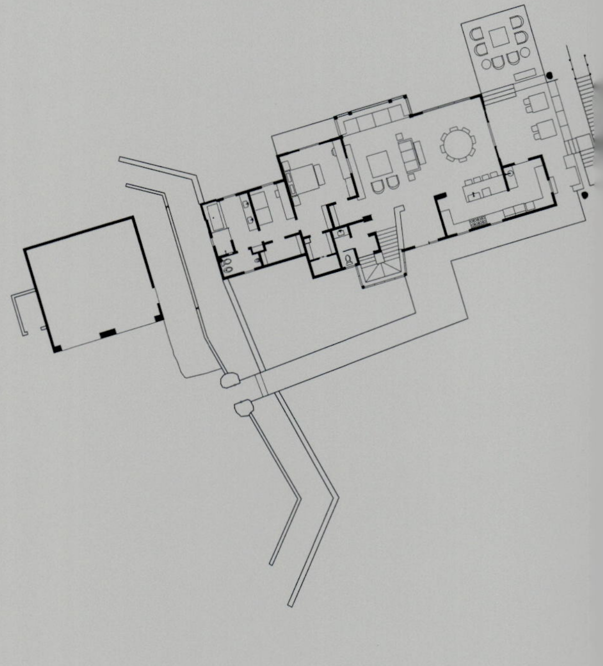

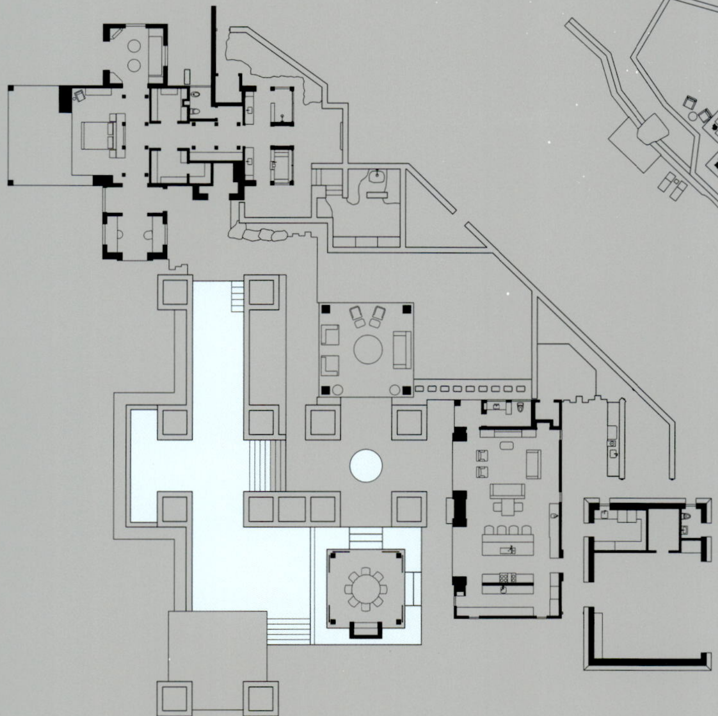
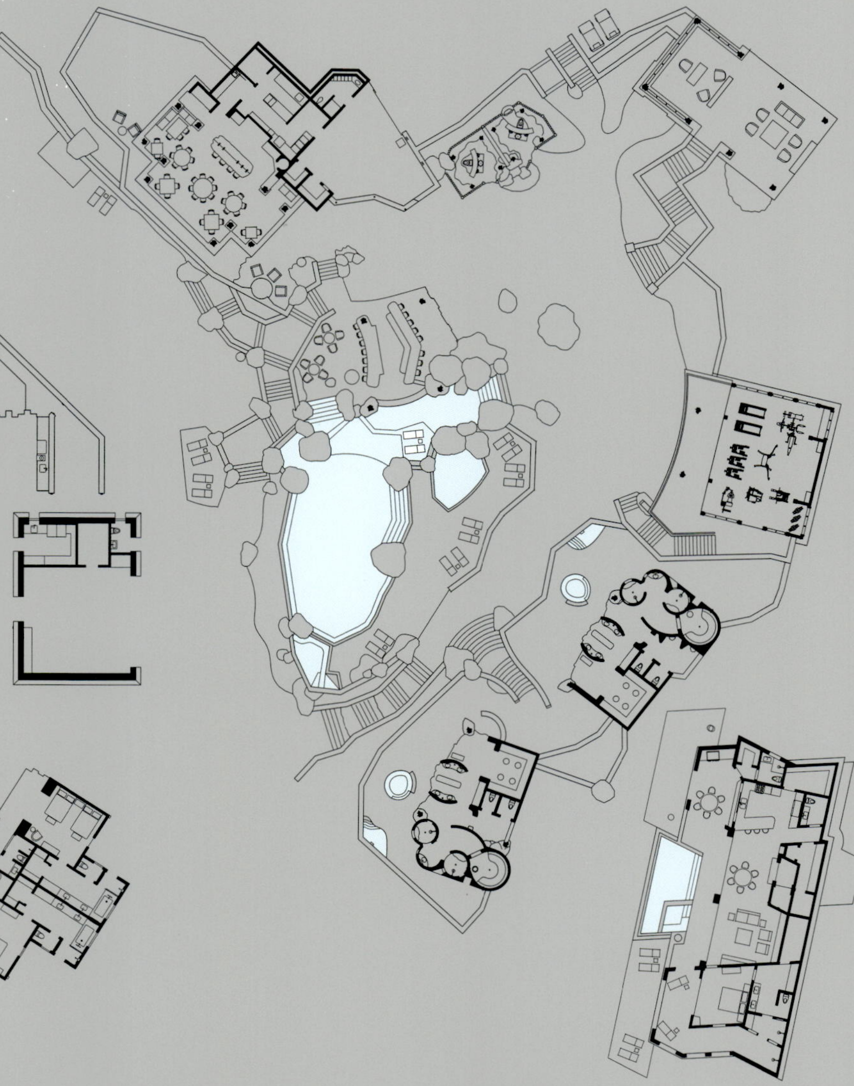
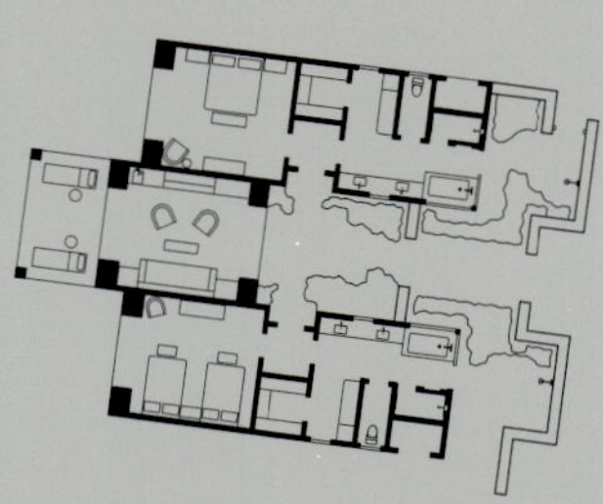
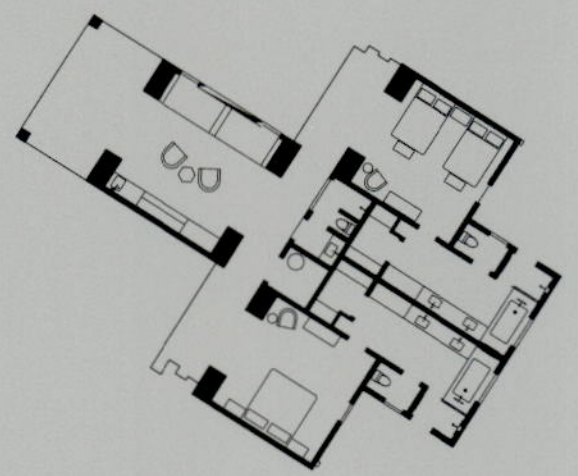

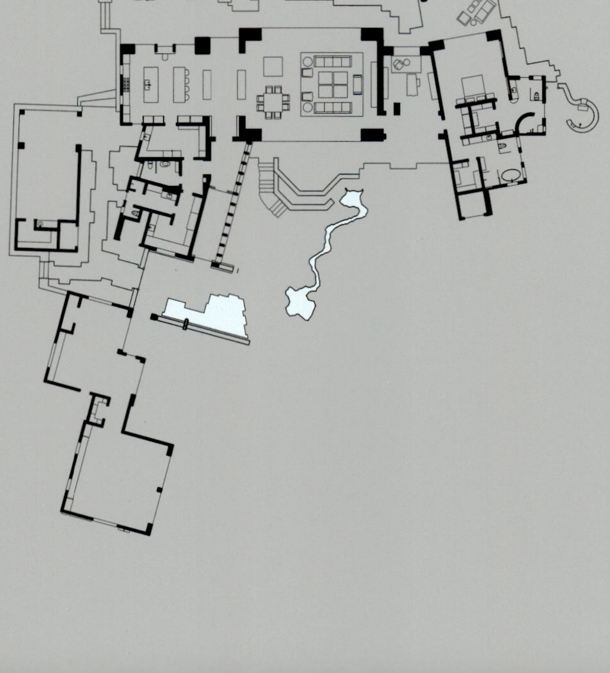

ORO Editions
Publishers of Architecture, Art, and Design
Publisher: Gordon Goff

www.oroeditions.com
info@oroeditions.com

Published by ORO Editions

Copyright © 2022 de Reus Architects, Inc.

All rights reserved. No part of this book may be reproduced, stored in a retrieval system, or transmitted in any form or by any means, including electronic, mechanical, photocopying of microfilming, recording, or otherwise (except that copying permitted by Sections 107 and 108 of the U.S. Copyright Law and except by reviewers for the public press) without written permission from the publisher.

You must not circulate this book in any other binding or cover and you must impose this same condition on any acquirer.

Managing Editor: Gordon Goff

Project Editor and Book Design: Pablo Mandel
Typeset in Avenir

10 9 8 7 6 5 4 3 2 1 First Edition

ISBN: 978-1-951541-24-8

Color Separations and Printing: ORO Group Ltd.
Printed in China.

ORO Editions makes a continuous effort to minimize the overall carbon footprint of its publications. As part of this goal, ORO Editions, in association with Global ReLeaf, arranges to plant trees to replace those used in the manufacturing of the paper produced for its books. Global ReLeaf is an international campaign run by American Forests, one of the world's oldest nonprofit conservation organizations. Global ReLeaf is American Forests' education and action program that helps individuals, organizations, agencies, and corporations improve the local and global environment by planting and caring for trees.